AGILE
PROJECT
MANAGEMENT

AGILE PROJECT MANAGEMENT

How to Succeed in the Face of Changing Project Requirements

Gary Chin

AMACOM

American Management Association

New York • Atlanta • Brussels • Chicago • Mexico City • San Francisco
Shanghai • Tokyo • Toronto • Washington, D.C.

Special discounts on bulk quantities of AMACOM books are available to corporations, professional associations, and other organizations. For details, contact Special Sales Department, AMACOM, a division of American Management Association, 1601 Broadway, New York, NY 10019.
Tel.: 212-903-8316.   Fax: 212-903-8083.
Web site: www.amacombooks.org

Library of Congress Cataloging-in-Publication Data

Chin, Gary.
        Agile project management : how to succeed in the face of changing project requirements / Gary Chin.
            p.   cm.
        Includes index.
        ISBN 0-8144-7176-5
        1. Project management.   I. Title.
HD69.P75C469   2004
658.4'04—dc22
                                                                2003022111

Printing number

10   9   8   7   6   5   4   3   2   1

CONTENTS

PREFACE

Today's innovative minds are constantly pushing the envelope: New and often disruptive technologies are filling the product development pipelines of both large and small companies. The business landscape is fast-paced and competitive, and product lifecycles are shorter. Naturally, product development and launch times are also shortening as companies aggressively develop new products and services to compete. This emphasis on speed forces teams to make quick decisions with incomplete information or in an environment of uncertainty. This, in turn, leads to frequent changes in project requirements and direction. Teams need to be light on their feet . . . they need to be agile!

The need for agility is magnified in highly innovative businesses that are pushing the limits of current technology and thinking, and where key parts of projects often involve discovery or problem solving never encountered before. These types of projects have an inherent uncertainty and involve multiple paths, decision points, and iterations before they can be successfully completed. Technical teams know that it is impossible to precisely plan new discoveries far in advance. Consequently, they only use project management for administrative support, if they use it at all. Their resistance to using project management is, in fact, often valid. The classical project management technique that they have experienced is cumbersome and not as effective in a fast-paced and uncertain environment. Additionally, project management is more often than not perceived as bureaucratic overhead that will probably slow the team down rather than make it more agile. While I don't fully agree with this viewpoint, I see that many of the commonly known PM practices and tools are geared toward large and relatively slow-moving projects.

On a broader scale, companies realize that they must continue to change and remake themselves to remain competitive—to hit their financial targets and drive the business forward. These business-level changes include not only developing new products and services, but also creating the innovative HR practices, marketing messages, partnerships, acquisitions, and reorganizations that will keep them ahead of the competition. In all of these cases, projects are the engines that power the business transformation and, in turn, enable the organizational flexibility necessary to survive in today's world. To this end, most companies recognize that effective and *agile* project management is essential for their survival. The problem is getting there!

Modern project management, as developed in the post–World War II era, was initially employed to manage large government projects for the military and construction and space industries. It has subsequently evolved and been widely adopted in some form by most large commercial companies. Nowadays, these same project management techniques are well on their way into many medium and small companies. However, as you may guess, what works well for a huge government project may not be the optimal solution for an innovative start-up or even a smaller entrepreneurial group within a large company. Those early projects had many unique challenges, such as efficiently managing hundreds of subcontractors, that project management was able to address. The ability to meet these challenges created the momentum that carried project management into the mainstream.

While many of these original characteristics are still present in today's projects, most have evolved along with business in general, and some have changed radically. For the most part, the science of project management has kept pace with the evolution of business over the past few decades. However, in certain areas, project management has not evolved in step with business and therefore cannot effectively address its challenges. It is some of these areas that are the focus of this book.

If we fast-forward from 1950 to 2004, we will notice a dramatic economic shift in business—an increase in the number of small companies versus large companies. This shift was driven largely by the advent of the knowledge-based economy. At one time, only large companies with significant financial capital controlled the resources required to compete in business. Their resources were physical assets, such as buildings, material, and equipment. As knowledge and intellectual property became increasingly more valuable assets, entrepreneurs with little financial capital but significant intellectual capital were able to start small businesses and carve out niches in this new market space.

In their quest to grow and compete, these smaller businesses are looking to PM as a possible competitive advantage. They realize that good PM can add tremendous value to their projects; however, they also recognize that the familiar, classic PM approach is not quite right for them. Yet, they press on, with the understanding that their PM processes will have to undergo optimization over time.

The organizations that need new ideas in (agile) project management the most are likely to be investing the least in developing them.

There are a few subtle points related to this evolution that are worth noting. First, the sponsors and managers of projects generally know that one-size project management does not fit all, so they look to tailor classic PM processes to their particular situation. This approach will address some, but not all, of their challenges. Second, specialized and dedicated process development resources are required to develop, implement, and maintain robust project management processes, especially ones tuned to a unique and dynamic environment. Third, these process development resources quickly dwindle as company size shrinks, yet this is where customized project management processes have perhaps the biggest impact.

In some ways, project management has become a more or less rote mechanical process because it has been proven to work effectively on more or less rote mechanical projects. However, when applied to the more creative, uncertain, and urgent projects, classic PM practices often falter and need assistance. It is in these situations where we will explore various new thinking that will supplement the current body of knowledge on project management and, hopefully, extend its effectiveness into agile environments.

Acknowledgment

For my wonderful family, Cara, Maddie, and Garrett, who gave me the time and support to write this book, and whom I love dearly. Also, thanks to my friends Mark and Anne, who provided encouragement and helped me think through the many details.

1

DEFINING AGILE PROJECT MANAGEMENT

Those of you who have managed projects in a technology environment know that balancing the needs of the project management (PM) process against those of a creative technical team is something of an art. You risk stifling innovation with too much process. With too little process, you risk never getting the project completed. The mismatch occurs when you try to employ classic PM methods in an agile environment. While many companies have spent significant money and energy customizing common PM processes to their specific situations, they are still finding that it is more of an art than a science, where certain project managers thrive and others struggle. Building on classic PM methods can take you only so far in the uncertain environment that's so typical of projects pushing the boundaries of technological and business innovation. Agile PM will provide some new concepts and techniques that I've seen to be effective in dynamic environments and that, hopefully, will help you advance your project management foundation in these challenging areas.

Overextension

A primary reason that expanding on classic PM methods is not as effective in certain areas is that it is simply being overstretched. Over the years, classic PM has evolved into a wide and solid platform for delivering all sorts of projects in all kinds of environments. People have taken comprehensive, classic PM methods and customized them for their unique situations. In turn, this has further validated and expanded the classic PM platform. I have yet to encounter a company that hasn't done some type of PM customization for its specific business, yet the core methods always come back to the classic fundamentals. However, like any platform, classic PM has its constraints, and as we stretch it to address the new scenarios that lie on the fringe of the platform edges, it becomes less effective (see Figure 1-1). It is in these fringe areas at the edge of the classic PM platform that agile PM comes into play.

As you continue to advance your project management methods to keep pace with your changing project and business requirements, it is generally easier to build off an established idea or concept, rather than starting from scratch. In the agile environment, the problem is that there isn't a good foundation to start from because classic project management has been overextended. This book will attempt to correct that situation. Agile PM can be viewed as a new foundation element, perhaps just a single post, that will help support the extensions of the classic PM platform in such a way as to enable its practitioners to more effectively manage projects in an uncertain environment.

Planning Versus Execution

When the term *project management* is mentioned, the image that most often pops to mind is that of the Gantt chart, also known as the project timeline or schedule. From an academic perspective, we know that project management encompasses the end-to-end project lifecycle. Yet in practical application, there's a strong emphasis on the *planning* stage, perhaps at the expense of other important process areas. This is partially due to the focus on planning by the affordable project management software applications, as well as the proven track record of solid planning over the past decades. However, as project and business environments become more dynamic, the effective planning horizon

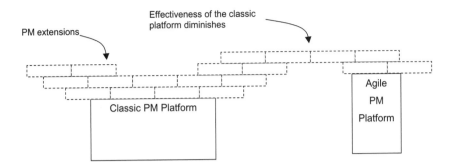

Figure 1-1. The relationship between classic and agile PM platforms.

becomes shorter. If we insist on holding fast to our planning-focused approach to project management and do not recognize the shifting horizon, we will be setting ourselves up for failure and frustration.

In the agile environment, the PM emphasis is moved from *planning* to *execution*. It is during project execution that crucial decisions are made that determine success or failure of the project. This is not to say that the areas of project definition and planning will be ignored, just that their focus will shift to supporting decisions during project execution rather than making them all up-front.

The Characteristics of Agile Project Management

In this book, I define agile environments as those that exhibit internal and/or external uncertainty, may require some unique expertise, and possess a high level of urgency. A more specific way of defining the agile PM environment is as follows:

Agile PM Environment = [Uncertainty + Unique Expertise] × Speed

Project uncertainty is the primary factor making the case for agile PM. Secondly, if your project requires unique expertise, it can also benefit from agile PM. This expertise may be represented by the sole individual who understands how all the pieces of a project fit together technically, such as the system architect, or by the most knowledgeable person in a small but critical area. The need for speed, which I call a multiplying factor, is the third and final component of an environment conducive to agile PM. When combined in varying degrees, these three characteristics, especially uncertainty, can create an environment of changing project requirements. Most project managers know from experience that it is difficult at best, and frustrating at worst, to successfully run a project where the requirements are dynamic. Yet this is the world that many of us live in, and it is the world where the agile PM techniques described in this book will be most applicable.

There are two types of project uncertainty that we will discuss in this book—internal and external.

❏ *Internal uncertainty* involves those things under the project umbrella that can be more or less controlled by the project manager, including scope, schedule, and cost.

❏ *External uncertainty* involves those factors not under the project umbrella, such as the industry's business environment, the competition, and high-level, business strategy decisions.

Both are critical elements to consider, but one or the other may be more prevalent in any particular project. This, in turn, will help determine how you deal with them.

Internal Uncertainty

Let's look at internal uncertainty first. Some projects may be considered essentially the same as, or at least very similar to, previous projects undertaken by the company. Home or commercial construction, equipment installation, and maintenance come to mind as examples. Even if there are initially some internal unknowns, no matter what pops up, the team has probably already encountered a similar situation on past projects and thus will be able to minimize the impact on the overall project. An example might be the installation of a new piece of manufacturing equipment that upgrades a section of an active production line. This example represents an important project in that it boosts long-term capacity, it is critical that it be executed on time or it will impact short-term production requirements, and it involves unknowns, as this is a new piece of equipment. Yet, in reality, this project has minimal internal uncertainty. Live production lines have been successfully upgraded before. The team knows who needs to be involved, and it knows the potential impacts on all of the cross-functional areas. While there have been problems in the past, the team has learned from them. In essence, the team has the knowledge to pull together and execute a fairly comprehensive project plan. If anything unusual comes up, which it always seems to, the team is confident that, based on experience, it will be able to handle it. In essence, the internal uncertainty of a project is inversely proportional to the level of experience on similar ones (see Figure 1-2).

On the other hand, development projects, especially those involving scientific discovery, are totally different. Internal unknowns on these projects are usually plentiful, and they may create changes that take the project off its original course for good. Does this mean that you should give up on your original timelines and objectives? No. It means you have to be agile in making your course changes. You should expect that internal uncertainty of this type will have significant impact on the project, so it will have to be actively managed. An example might be a company's development of a new technology that will enable drug targeting for cancer medications. This project is im-

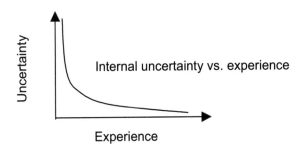

Figure 1-2. Internal uncertainty is higher when doing something for the first time, and it diminishes as you gain experience.

portant to the company because it has a potentially huge revenue impact. In addition to the core scientific team, there is a considerable extended team supporting the effort. However, this project has huge amounts of internal uncertainty because the company has never done this kind of development before. Furthermore, very few other people, if any, have ever done this kind of work before. While the team is comfortable with its scientific approach to this project, it doesn't really know what to expect down the road. Therefore, it is reluctant to develop and commit to a comprehensive project plan. The team readily expects some surprises as the project progresses, but it can't anticipate, with any reasonable level of certainty, how it will handle them.

Classic PM was initially developed around mature organizations that had wrung much of the internal uncertainty out of their business.

Generally, the more mature an organization or company, the less internal uncertainty it will have in its projects. By maturity, I essentially mean the length of time a company or organization has been in existence working in its area of expertise. Organizations that are experienced at their craft can usually manage projects with much more predictability because they have removed much of the uncertainty, or unknowns, from their projects. They have learned through trial and error and thus are less likely to repeat mistakes. While not all mature organizations are necessarily large, most large organizations are relatively mature. Almost by definition, large organizations have gained maturity as they grew, and it was here that formal project management methods first took hold.

External Uncertainty

Because this area is largely outside the project manager's control, it is not usually observed in great detail. Nevertheless, it is areas external to the actual project that have, perhaps, the greatest influence on its outcome. As we will discuss later, project managers who successfully work in an agile environment will turn much of their attention away from the project itself and toward the external influences that may blow it off course. The project manager usually cannot control real external forces to his project but, if agile enough, can make the appropriate adjustments to keep the project objectives in sight.

The amount of influence that external uncertainty has on your project is largely determined by the industry in which you operate (see Figure 1-3). Industries that are relatively stable (i.e., where the focus is on evolutionary improvements rather than revolutionary ones) will see less external uncertainty. For instance, wholesale consumer-product distribution could be considered an industry that operates in a more or less foreseeable environment. Through proven banking relationships, this industry's financing picture is secure. Companies in this area have long-standing relationships with their customers, and they have a good understanding of the competition. The new technologies that may influence them are focused on efficiency improvements, not radical new thinking that can turn the industry upside down. In a nutshell, their business is fairly predictable.

On the other hand, industries that are emerging, or are in the process of remaking themselves, will exhibit signs of external uncer-

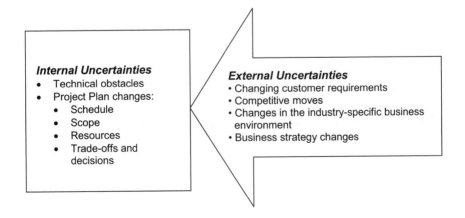

Figure 1-3. Project uncertainty is made up of both internal and external components.

tainty. For example, the Internet industry continues to emerge and expand at a fascinating rate. The endless list of potential Internet advancements must all be tried for the first time, and then optimized, all while the underlying and interlinked technology platform that supports the Internet is, itself, changing. The telecommunications sector is an example of an industry remaking itself to remain in step with new technologies such as wireless, voice over IP, instant messaging, PDAs, and even picture phones. Companies playing in this sector must cope with the ups and downs of the financial markets, the unstable technology infrastructure, and fierce competition.

Unlike internal uncertainty, which is more a function of company maturity, external uncertainty is largely a function of industry maturity. Generally, mature industries have weeded out much of the competition and have also erected barriers to entry for newcomers, thus reducing external uncertainty. Emerging industries have many new and smaller companies vying for position, which, in turn, causes a lot of rapid change and thus external uncertainty. However, the dynamics of the business world don't allow us to easily divide industries into two groups labeled "mature" and "immature." At any given time, some entrepreneur is working on a new and disruptive technology that could potentially upset the balance of a seemingly mature industry and, in the process, create a lot of external uncertainty for the entrenched players. When this happens, tried-and-true, classic project management practices may start to exhibit some difficulties. As more and more uncertainty is introduced to the previously mature and stable industry, the classic PM methods are stretched further and further. At some point, you will need to start looking for new ways to be running projects. Hopefully, you will find some of those new methods in *Agile Project Management.*

Unique Expertise

Projects that have their roots in innovation often require the use of unique expertise. At the heart of most innovative companies are the brilliant minds that drive the ideas and projects. These gurus often contribute significantly to many project areas. Unlike classic project management, where resources within a pool are interchangeable, there are no substitutes for the guru's unique expertise. Making the optimal use of unique expertise is part of agile PM.

Large corporations generally have a relatively large resource pool at their disposal. For example, when a project requires five electrical design engineers, the project planners can assume that electrical engineers (EEs) are a mostly homogeneous bunch (apologies to my many EE friends). If twenty-five of these engineers are employed by the company, then about 20 percent of them will need to be allocated to the project for its duration. If one engineer leaves for some reason, then (for planning purposes) any of the remaining engineers can probably be assigned to fill the gap.

Smaller companies, of course, have fewer resources, which tends to make them less homogeneous overall since a diversity of skills is still required to run the company. For companies driving innovation, the contrast is even more striking. Projects, and sometimes entire businesses, are formed around the unique skills of a single guru (or small number of gurus).

Speed

A lot has been written about how to move projects along faster by crashing the schedule, overlapping stage gates, or fast-tracking. These are all valid and valuable techniques. However, by this book's definition, being agile does not solely equate to being fast. Speed—or more appropriately, quickness—is a multiplying factor of agile PM, but not nearly the whole thing.

> **"Agile" does not equal "fast" in agile PM. However, speed is a multiplying factor of agility.**

Getting projects done faster is a universal desire of management everywhere. So, while nearly all projects are being pushed to move faster, the real urgency is not the same across the board, thus we need to look at it in relative terms. A project coming in late for a small start-up can literally mean the end of the company. If it can't deliver on time, the start-up may run out of money, and that's it—game over! On the other hand, while large company management may push project managers to deliver on a tight timeline, the bottom line is that the impact of a late project on a big company is relatively small. It is not going to go out of business, and it will be able to make the appropriate adjustments to continue to steer forward.

This dynamic of urgency is partially driven by financial security, but it is also directly driven by the level of competition. Companies that feel the threat of competition breathing down their necks certainly have some urgency to execute projects faster. Speed is one tool to fight off competitors. Those that do not have that threat will not feel the urgency associated with it. For example, when a company with a dominant market position decides to upgrade its product, it doesn't have to worry much about racing to the finish line since there really isn't anyone to race against. The presence of competition creates urgency, which, in turn, creates pressure to move projects faster. Speeding up projects has been an area of project management focus for some time; however, when combined with other agile project characteristics, it takes on a new perspective.

The reality of project management is that you never really have the time to create the perfect plan, to analyze all the options, to get buy-in on decisions from all the stakeholders, etc. As the pressure mounts to move ever faster, plans are created and decisions are made with less and less information, creating an environment of uncertainty. So, while you may intuitively think that there is minimal project uncertainty, when combined with the pressure to move fast, it can actually become quite significant (see Figure 1-4).

The Focus of This Book

The science of project management is constantly growing and changing to meet the many diverse needs of projects everywhere. The various levels of government, nonprofit organizations, and private-sector

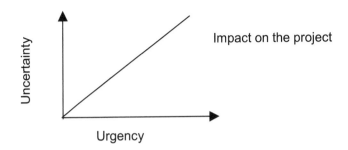

Figure 1-4. Impact of uncertainty on the project as a function of urgency.

companies all run projects. The organizations range in size from the very large to the very small, as do the projects. Finally, there are many unique industries, all with their own project management characteristics. To cover all of these permutations would require a vast text, and it probably would not be very practical.

My feeling is that there is opportunity for advancing project management in those areas that are rife with uncertainty. The goal of this book is to give you some actionable ideas that will help you to better manage projects in these areas.

Agile Project Management provides some core project management methods, but it also looks at how organizations should use project management to become more effective and successful businesses. These concepts need to be taken and customized to your unique business environment. Since agile PM permeates so many project areas, I will be focusing as much on "what" to do as "how" to do it. Moreover, the "what" to do for agile PM is much more than just what the project manager should be doing. It includes understanding the business drivers, developing the right project management infrastructure, and nurturing a supportive project management environment. I'll also review the roles of the project manager, the project team, and management, and look at how they need to adapt to achieve agile PM.

Summary

❑ Classic PM is becoming overextended as we try to apply it to the agile project environment.

❑ Classic PM was largely developed by organizations that had wrung much of the uncertainty out of their business during a time of less competition and, therefore, less project urgency.

❑ Four dimensions drive the need for agile PM: internal uncertainty, external uncertainty, the use of unique expertise, and speed/ urgency.

2

DETERMINING WHEN TO USE AGILE PROJECT MANAGEMENT

Agile project management concepts are not for every project, yet they can be invaluable to others. So, how do you know which agile ideas are best applied to your situation?

Agile project management is not an all-or-nothing methodology. You should examine ways of combining classic and agile PM concepts where each makes the most sense. Classic project management is very comprehensive, and it has been proven to work in diverse project situations. Agile project management adds new ideas for addressing the unique project situations formed out of creative, knowledge-based industries.

You will benefit if your project operates in an environment of high uncertainty. You probably will not gain much if you operate in a very predictable environment. (But who does that?) The truth is that you are probably somewhere in between, where you will benefit from some ideas but not others. This chapter discusses two key project criteria that, together, will help you quickly surmise the applicability of agile PM concepts to your particular situation, as well as the potential value it may add to your organization.

Criterion 1: Project Environments

Over the years, I've encountered three different types of project environments within the technology and scientific areas. They are the operational environment, the product/process development environment, and the technology development environment. The operational environment is fairly predictable (i.e., low uncertainty), while both the technology and product/process development environments are more unpredictable (i.e., higher uncertainty). There is, of course, some overlap between these broad categories, but understanding generally where your situation fits will help you determine the extent to which agile PM concepts will benefit your project.

The Operational Project Environment

Let's start with the operational project environment (see Figure 2-1). By operational, I mean those projects that are run with a regular frequency, are very similar to each other, and are critical to the day-to-day running of the business. Service provisioning is a good example of the operational project environment. Setting up a customer for a new service, either as a one-time user or on an ongoing basis, can be a significant project to do properly. However, the general workflow is basically the same for each customer. Contract manufacturing is another example of this type of project environment. While each product may be unique, the process for building out and running the manufacturing systems is common across all products.

These types of projects are fairly regular, and the organization knows how to do them because it has done many others in the past.

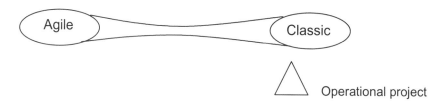

Figure 2-1. The operational project environment is more conducive to classic PM.

Because the level of uncertainty is low, these projects are often better served by classic methods, which are more process-oriented.

The Technology Development Project Environment

Next, let's look at the projects at the opposite end of the spectrum—those focused on the development of a new technology (see Figure 2-2). I am not talking about a new product or application, but rather the development of breakthrough technology, upon which future products will be built. As such, these developments are often referred to as technology platforms. They often become the basis for entirely new companies or industries. Technology development projects are very unique in nature. There is no template project teams can work from and, in fact, a project management template, or any template for that matter, may greatly restrict the team creativity required to create such a new technology platform.

Agile PM is most applicable in the technology/platform development project environment.

These early-stage, groundbreaking projects have never been done before under the same circumstances. The level of internal uncertainty is high. The team requires creativity, determination, and commitment. The project management environment, in turn, needs to support the team's needs and not conflict with them. The general approach to these projects is vastly different from the way the team would ap-

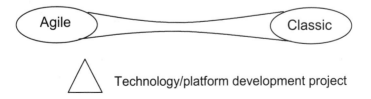

Figure 2-2. The technology development project environment is more conducive to agile PM.

proach something that it has done before. The team will likely need
to pursue multiple pathways and iterations as it progresses toward its
end goal (unlike the more classic approach of focusing on a single,
primary, critical path). Agile project management can provide great
value in these situations.

The Product/Process Development Project Environment

Finally, let's examine a project situation somewhere in the middle—
the product/process development project (see Figure 2-3). While the
product/process may be unique, the technology platform is usually
already in place, and a well-defined product development process
(PDP) is most likely utilized. In the large corporation, product development projects can be complex, cross-functional efforts with many
stakeholders, or in a small business, they may be the center of the
entire company. While the pure technology development project involves mostly a scientific and engineering team, product/process development involves less front-end science/engineering expertise and
more business acumen. Therefore, marketing and manufacturing are
usually involved because of their know-how in bringing products to
market. These kinds of projects still require a great deal of engineering
creativity, yet they must balance those needs with the discipline required to launch and maintain successful products or services.

These types of projects can also have a relatively high level of
uncertainty, especially for those companies in the high-tech and scientific industries. In addition to the scientific uncertainties associated
with the technology development project, product/process development must deal with business and market uncertainties, which are clas-

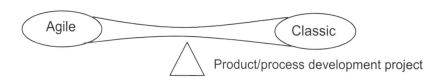

Figure 2-3. The product development project environment requires a mix of classic PM
and agile PM.

sified here as external uncertainties. Since there are many varied perspectives on the cross-functional team, agile PM can create value both by helping to navigate around uncertainty and by providing a mechanism for pulling together diverse teams. Additionally, while product development projects really need a combination of both classic and agile techniques, there is considerable opportunity for applying agile methods, since these comprise such a large percentage of projects in the innovative space.

Criterion 2: Organizational Stakeholders

The second project dimension that will help you determine the applicability of agile concepts is your type of organizational stakeholders. Specifically, do they include customers, partners, and subcontractors? The agile PM concepts in this book revolve largely around how the organization applies its project management efforts. In addition to addressing specific tools and processes, agile PM is concerned with organizational dynamics and attitudes. In concrete terms, what this means is that agile PM concepts have the best chance of success when the project operates under, more or less, a single organizational umbrella (see Figure 2-4.)

The Single Organization

An early-stage technology development project may have widespread potential applications but no specific external customer. The only real customer of the project is the business that is sponsoring it. This project is likely to be undertaken in its entirety within the company, per-

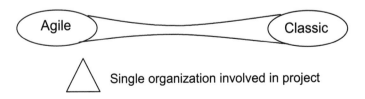

Figure 2-4. Agile PM is more applicable when there are fewer organizational stakeholders.

haps only within R&D, and thus there are no partners or subcontractors on the team. In essence, there is a single organizational umbrella under which the project resides and, hopefully, there are common project objectives for the team. By operating under a single organizational umbrella, you will have a much better chance of creating an agile project environment in which to operate than if you had multiple stakeholder organizations to deal with.

Multiple Organizations

At the other extreme is the project that spans multiple, distinct organizations. While it is not impossible to create a successful agile environment across multiple organizations, it will be significantly more challenging. At this end of the spectrum, classic PM techniques are often more appropriate because they do a good job of setting expectations for multiple stakeholders, which include all of the distinct, external customers, partners, and subcontractors (see Figure 2-5). Since projects are, by definition, of finite duration, it often doesn't make sense to try to create an agile PM environment across multiple corporate cultures. The time and effort required to create the agile culture may not have time to pay off, depending on the length of the project. Additionally, when many different companies are involved, it is unlikely that they will all have the common objectives required for ultimate project success within the agile paradigm. The chief reason for this is money. Everyone will be working to ensure that they get paid their fair share, as they should. Under a single organization, it is easier to justify sacrifices in one area for the good of the overall project.

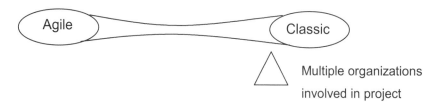

Figure 2-5. Classic PM is more applicable when there are multiple organizational stakeholders.

However, it is unlikely that one subcontractor will agree to work significantly more than originally planned without additional compensation for the benefit of the other subcontractors or even for the overall project.

Agile project management cuts across organizational boundaries to confront and constructively address complex interactions and interfaces.

This does not mean that agile concepts are totally inapplicable in this type of project situation. You should just be judicious in deciding which concepts to use. You should be aware of the challenges of driving environmental change across multiple organizations. For multiyear projects, or for situations where there is a strong, prime contractor that can drive organizational change across subcontractors, agile PM may be a powerful tool you can use to gain a competitive advantage.

Single Company, Multiple Organizations

The in-between case is when a project operates within a single corporate umbrella, but where the divisions or functional areas involved operate as, more or less, autonomous organizations with their own objectives (see Figure 2-6). Depending on how the leaders of these organizations are motivated, it could be easy (or difficult) to introduce agile PM concepts. This is where most technology projects that can benefit from agile PM reside, and thus, it is an area with a strong potential return.

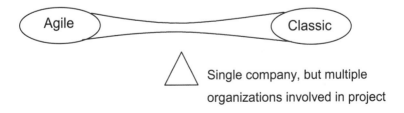

Figure 2-6. Both agile and classic PM may be applicable when there are multiple organizations within a single company.

Since projects are a very visible mechanism that cut across multiple organizations, they also have the unique ability to influence organizational effectiveness across the entire business. Projects bring out the organizational dynamics that are not seen when one looks at the business from a strictly operational view. Nonstandard interfaces and complex interactions surface. How the organization learns to deal with these situations can determine the long-term success or failure of the business itself. Agile project management identifies these organizational complexities and confronts them constructively within the project management paradigm. While the immediate goal is enhanced project performance, the ultimate objective of agile PM is increased organizational performance.

Deciding to employ agile PM is not a simple, black-and-white question. As you read this book, you will see that there are several areas that affect, and are affected by, agile PM concepts. Some of these areas will be very applicable to your unique situation and others will not. Agile PM is about new perspectives and techniques around project management. It is a culture-changing concept that may take patience to employ, but it will be worth the effort.

This chapter has provided some guidelines to help you understand how well agile PM may apply to your project situations by looking at two key project dimensions—the type of project environment and the organizational stakeholders. Figure 2-7 will help you quickly identify whether agile PM is suitable for your situation.

	Multiple, External Stakeholders	Multiple, Internal Stakeholders	Single Organization
Operational Projects	Classic	Classic	Classic
Product/Process Development Projects	Classic/Agile	Classic/Agile	Agile
Technology/Platform Development Projects	Classic/Agile	Agile	Agile

Figure 2-7. Applicability of agile PM, based on project type and organizational stakeholders.

Summary

❑ When assessing your project situation for the applicability of agile PM concepts, consider two key dimensions:

1. *Project Type.* Is it an operational, product/process development, or technology/platform development project?

2. *Type of Organizational Stakeholders.* Is there a single organization? Multiple, distinct organizations? Or is the project a hybrid involving both kinds of stakeholders?

3

PROJECTS ARE THE BUSINESS

In large companies, at any given time, there will be a number of projects taking place across various parts of the business. Some of these projects will span multiple internal organizations and some will be wholly contained within a single department. In essence, the management, project managers, and project team members consider these projects as part of the business. Individually, these projects will impact some part of the business, but probably will not have substantial impact on the overall business, whether they fail or are successful. As you might expect, this situation is much different for smaller organizations, especially those involved with developing new technologies. In these cases, a single project or small set of projects can define a majority of the total business. It doesn't really matter if it's a start-up business or an emerging business unit within a corporate giant. These organizations must deliver concrete results to survive. Success or failure of these projects can make or break the business. It is in these situations that we can no longer think of projects as part of the business. We must be thinking of the projects *as* the business!

Business Organization

If you look at the makeup of a typical business, it contains two broad parts (see Figure 3-1). The first is an *operational* part that performs

Operations	Projects
❑ Sales	❑ Technology development
❑ Manufacturing	❑ Product development
❑ Procurement	❑ Process development
❑ Distribution	❑ Product/service launch
❑ Billing	❑ Business process reengineering
❑ Technical support	❑ New capability development

Figure 3-1. Typical business consisting of operational and project elements.

routine day-to-day activities that are related to generating revenue, such as manufacturing, sales, or billing. The second is the *project* part that focuses on the future vision for the company and may include R&D, marketing programs, and business process improvements.

In very general terms, products, services, and processes get created on the project side of the business and are transferred to the operations side of the business. The trick is to facilitate an efficient transfer from one side to the other or, ideally, to have hardly any transfer at all because the two sides are so well integrated. This chapter looks at some tactics for deeply integrating key projects into the overall business to the point where the project team becomes fully attuned to benefits of success and consequences of failure.

The Triple Constraint

In classic PM, projects are treated as distinct entities within the business. They have a scope, resources, and a schedule that are more or less self-contained. The project manager must work within these boundaries, sometimes referred to as the triple constraint or iron triangle of project management, to deliver the expected results. Any decisions that require changing one of these boundaries must come from outside of the project—typically from functional or executive management. For example, if something unexpected happens that requires changing one of the boundaries (i.e., either the scope, resources, or schedule), then the project manager collects all of the relevant information and brings the issue to the project sponsor. The sponsor, in turn, listens to the situation and takes the recommendations of the project manager under advisement. Before making a decision on how to proceed, the sponsor may add new information to the mix, confer with her peers, or bring it to the next level of management. This whole data collection, analysis, escalation, and decision-making process usually takes time, during which the project may be stalled.

This process is valid in many industries, especially mature ones where much of the uncertainty has been removed from the decision-making process by years of experience. In this case, the management decision makers are hopefully seasoned veterans with their finger on the pulse of the business's finances and market environment. Taking the time to prepare an in-depth analysis for management will likely pay off in the long run on the operational side of the business in areas such as lower production costs, lower support costs, and better overall product quality.

Now let's take a look at a company operating in an environment of internal and external uncertainty but that is trying to apply classic PM methods. The project comes to a decision point, but the project manager sees no obvious answer from his perspective. He starts collecting data so that he can create an analysis to present to the sponsor. However, in this environment there are limited solid facts upon which to build an analysis. This leads him to make educated assumptions, perhaps based on the consensus opinion of his team, which takes additional time. At the completion of the analysis, he notices that there are multiple possible paths with no clear "best option" to recommend. Oh well, perhaps management has additional information that will help make the decision? And he's right. Management does add new information to the equation, but they also add some external uncertainties. The analysis now has so many dimensions and possible outcomes that it becomes nearly useless. Yet somehow, a decision is finally made and the project progresses.

Let's examine what just happened. To make a mediocre decision, the project manager involved himself, a good part of his team, and management. This is both time-consuming and an inefficient use of resources, especially since the same decision, or perhaps a better one, could have been made a lot quicker if the project manager had access to the right information from the start and was allowed to look "outside his box" (i.e., his triple constraint) to make the decision.

In the classic PM model, the project manager is basically put into a box, albeit, a triangular box. He is usually given considerable liberty to operate within the box but very little leeway to work outside it, which is where traditional management gets involved. Even if no explicit directions are given to the project manager, it is human nature to focus on things within one's control, which again is inside the box.

For the large, complex company, this makes pretty good sense. It is only logical that a large organization requiring numerous distinct roles in order to operate should create a *project manager* role to run the project and a *management* role to set the boundaries for the project. However, if freed from the complexity constraint inherent in large organizations, would you still choose these distinct roles for your company?

I would argue that while the natural evolution of project management has created these project boxes that cut across the functional silos of large companies, this is not the most agile way to organize projects for smaller organizations. While this model works for corporate giants in mature industries, it falls apart badly as you move to the opposite end of the PM agility spectrum—where speed is required and uncertainty abounds.

Agile Strategy

View your projects in the same perspective as your business, by integrating project and business decision-making processes, and you will better achieve your business objectives.

Equating the Project and the Business

To start, we need to view projects as the business, or at least a core part of the business. This means figuring out how to integrate project and business decision making. When you are running a business in a fast-paced, competitive environment filled with unknowns, isolating your project teams inside boxes is like driving blind. More than just opening a window to look outside the project, we need to fully integrate the project with the business strategy, other related projects, and key operational activities. In a small company, this may involve reorganizing the whole business around a single core project. In a larger company, it may require deeper integration among the project, program, and business objectives.

Achieving this business and project integration involves both internal and external aspects (see Figure 3-2). Internal elements are those that reside within the sponsor organization, such as the high-level business objectives, other projects in the company's portfolio, and day-to-day operational activities that keep the business running. Ensuring that all of these efforts are, in fact, supportive of each other requires that they are initially aligned and then that the alignment is maintained as decisions are made and the various elements change during project execution.

The external elements include your customers, competition, and any other influences external to your organization that may affect the project or the business. Information from external sources may enter the organization through your project team, a different project team, an operational area, or management or marketing and, quite often, stays in that small area of the organization. Getting this pertinent information to propagate throughout the organization is necessary for agility.

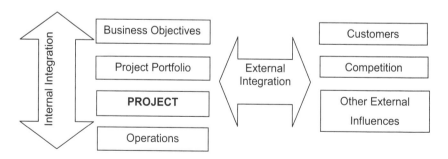

Figure 3-2. In agile PM, both the internal and external aspects of business and project decision making are integrated.

The first step in this direction is to enable, allow, and encourage project managers to look outside of their projects. Having an outward perspective is a powerful agile paradigm, yet very difficult to realize. Establishing an effective outward orientation is difficult because it involves developing a new project management infrastructure (to enable the outward view) and transforming your business environment (to allow and encourage the outward view). Both of these points will be discussed in more detail in Chapters 5 and 10, on the project manager's role and the operational infrastructure, respectively.

Agile Strategy

Have your project managers take more of an outward-facing perspective from their project, to facilitate the integration of the project and the business.

The primary reason that we need project managers to shift from an inward to an outward orientation is to get them more closely aligned with the real business objectives that the project is intended to achieve. This puts them in a position to feel the threat of competition and to understand the potential consequences of failure. An agile project needs to be more concerned with delivering results that solve business needs, rather than staying within preset project boundaries (see Figure 3-3). Project managers should be focused on beating the competition to market, developing new and unique product features, or making the best utilization of a rare resource. These goals put projects into the business context in a real way. The team is connected to the business outcome and therefore is better able to deliver results that contribute to the bottom line.

Agile Strategy

Focus your project manager's energy on delivering results that solve business needs rather than staying within preset project boundaries.

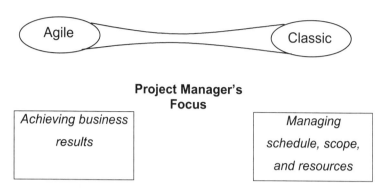

Figure 3-3. The primary focus of the project manager in an agile versus classic project environment.

One reason that the classic PM model of setting project constraints up-front works well in many situations is that the business objectives are matched to the project constraints at the start of the project. If the business environment is relatively stable, then the project constraints will remain aligned with the higher-level business objectives. However, in fast and uncertain environments where things tend to change, you may soon find that the original constraints no longer align with what's happening in the real world outside of the project. Then the reality is diverging from the box, and we need to decide whether the project is the box or if the *project is the business.*

In an uncertain environment, the original project boundaries will quickly diverge from the business reality.

As project boundaries (scope, schedule, resources) become more dynamic, the agile PM concept of integrating the project and the business becomes more applicable (see Figure 3-4). It should be pretty clear that decision making and thus project progress will be slowed if the management team needs to be constantly involved in redefining project boundaries.

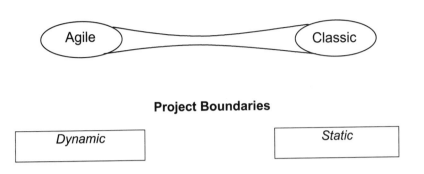

Figure 3-4. The predominately static project boundaries of the classic project give way to more dynamic conditions in the agile project.

There is no question that effective boundary management should be a cornerstone of all types of project management, classic or agile. A clear understanding of project boundaries is critical as projects are initiated and planned to ensure that the team knows what it is trying to accomplish (scope), by when (schedule), and with what means of support (resources). At closure, too, the team and sponsor need to know whether the project was successful. How the project team and the business organization approach boundary management during the project execution may differ, however.

In classic PM, the project manager is expected to execute course changes within the schedule, scope, and resources of the project, but not necessarily changes prompted by external events. This makes sense since the project manager has intimate knowledge of what's happening inside the project but not in the overall business environment. Other people in the company are charged with understanding the various parts of the business environment and communicating relevant events back to the project manager, if deemed necessary.

Agile PM strives to get these two camps integrated so that better decisions can be made in a more timely fashion (see Figure 3-5). The project team is then better able to adapt to the constantly changing requirements inherent in the agile environment. Looking at the project as the business is one way to enable that integration of project and business decision making. Having your project managers take an outward-facing perspective is another.

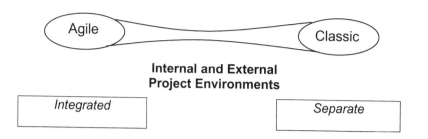

Figure 3-5. Agile PM looks to integrate the internal and external project environments.

Matrix Management and the Integration of Project and Business Decision Making

Matrix management is one of the most widely adopted approaches to managing projects. Its premise is to establish cross-functional teams, composed of representatives from stakeholder organizations, to run the projects (see Figure 3-6). These cross-functional team members belong to their respective functional organizations, report to the functional manager, and are "loaned" to the project manager for the purpose of completing the project. The idea is that a project team composed of the right diverse resources will be able to deliver the project better and more efficiently than a homogeneous team with no sense of ownership for project results. Concurrent engineering, a derivative of the matrix model, is a good example for product development projects where there is a relatively complex organization and many stakeholders working together on the same product. It has

	Functional Area #1	Functional Area #2	Functional Area #3	Functional Area #n
Project A				
Project B				
Project C				

Figure 3-6. Typical organizational structure for matrix management.

proved to be an effective practice for facilitating the transfer of work (from the project side to the operational side) and eliminating the old "throw it over the wall" product development mentality. Likewise, the matrix management concept has been very successful in larger companies with a fair amount of organizational complexity.

The matrix management model integrates the project with the business organization, but not with the business objectives.

While the matrix does help to facilitate the management of projects across multifunctional organizations, it can be a stumbling block in achieving true integration of business and project decision making, which we identified previously as a key to enabling project teams to view their project as the business. The benefits and challenges of matrix management are well known, and you may be thinking that the obvious thing to do is to migrate toward a "stronger matrix," where project managers wield more influence than functional managers. Even though this would seem to strengthen the position of the project, it still requires some type of balancing act and trade-offs with functional management.

By its very definition, the matrix approach to project management separates business and project decision making, creating an inherent inefficiency for those projects operating in an agile environment.

The matrixed approach to project management separates, rather than integrates, business and project decision making.

Perhaps the most recognized challenge of the matrix management structure is that project team members are put into the position of having two bosses—their functional manager and the project manager—thus potentially creating undercurrents of tension and confusion between team members, their manager, and the project manager. In organizational cultures where the functional and project managers have a mutual respect for each other, this arrangement works quite well. In fact, it may be the only somewhat efficient way to conduct projects in large companies. Additionally, matrix management has a sort of "political correctness" to it, in that it enables cross-functional projects to take place without reconfiguring the established functional organizational roles.

While the matrix organizational structure provides inherent efficiency for larger companies composed of numerous functional silos, it often adds unnecessary complexity to smaller businesses, which are more likely to be operating in an agile environment. Another potential problem with using the matrix approach in an agile environment is that small organizations often just don't have enough depth to adequately staff all the functional specialties that characterize a matrix approach. Consider the situation where a small business has a unique resource (guru) that is the heart and soul of the business. If this is the case, where do you put this key individual? Most companies give their star players positions at the head of a functional silo—after all, this is what we've been conditioned to aspire to in the big company model. However, what's more important to achieving the business objectives—heading up a functional department or executing key projects? Agile PM argues for the latter. Especially in smaller organizations, projects must be viewed as the business and therefore staffed with the key players necessary to make them successful.

We need to understand when the matrix is appropriate and when it is not. It is easy to default to the matrix mode since it is so commonly used, but this may not always be the best option for organizations at the fuzzy front-end (i.e., those pushing the limits of their field).

Upon review of the pros and cons of the matrix management approach (as outlined in Figure 3-7), we can see that while it is very appropriate for larger more mature businesses, it may not be the best choice for smaller, agile organizations that cannot reap the benefits and are hurt by its deficiencies.

Pros	Cons
Separates business and project decision making, therefore enabling better long-term decisions	Separates business and project decision making, therefore adding inefficiencies to project management
Tames the organizational and political complexities of large organizations	Creates unnecessary complexity for smaller organizations
Enables cross-functional projects to take place without reconfiguration of established roles	Creates tension and/or confusion by creating the "two bosses" environment
Enables focus on development of functional skills and processes	Doesn't make the best use of unique resources

Figure 3-7. The pros and cons of matrix management.

Agile Strategy

Switch from a matrix to a project-based organization if you don't have the depth to effectively staff a matrix and need to make the best use of key expertise, or if you need to better integrate project and business decision making.

The Project-Driven Organization

An alternative to the matrix organizational model is to create an organization around your key projects (see Figure 3-8). In this way, you develop a portfolio of projects that become your business. As technical project uncertainties create change from within, the business model adapts in turn. And when external influences force changes in the business, the project portfolio is able to more quickly absorb and compensate for the changes.

The project-driven organization is better suited to agile project environments (see Figure 3-9), with the key point being that business and project decision making are better integrated than in the matrix. The sole goal of project teams is to achieve the business objectives. The multiple, separate, and often conflicting objectives of the matrix

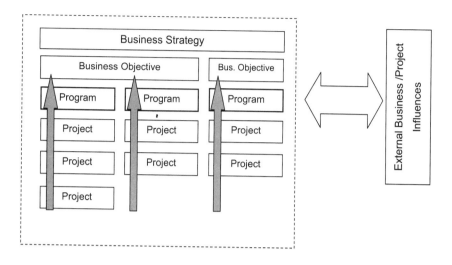

Figure 3-8. A project-based organization integrates the business strategy with the projects.

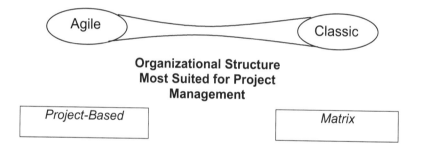

Figure 3-9. Project-based versus matrix organizations in agile and classic project environments.

organization don't exist. The silo mentality that so often inhibits project progress, especially when it involves changing requirements, is eliminated. Finally, your unique and key players can be put in place to guide your most important projects, the ones defining your business, without encountering obstacles from competing functional management.

Capitalizing on the strengths of your key personnel can be one of your strongest arguments for developing a project-driven organization. You can usually find ways to design your organization around your best performers, based on their specific skills, while still remaining on target with your higher-level objectives. This is not to say that you should be catering to the childish whims of a few eccentrics in your organization. However, you should be looking for ways to maximize their contribution and influence across your project set so it favorably impacts your ability to meet business objectives. After all, if your projects are your business and your key players are the heart and soul of your project, then it stands to reason that your key players are your business.

When there is a lot of energy spent on organization or silo building, as in the matrix model, it's easy to lose sight of the ball. If you play in an agile environment of constant change, then losing sight of your core strategies will be fatal. You need to document the key business objectives that will make you successful, define the projects necessary to execute on those objectives, and then fluently manage the change, whether it's driven by the projects or the external environment.

Agile Strategy

Keep your business strategies in sight by:

1. Defining your key business objectives

2. Defining a set of projects that will deliver on those objectives

3. Managing the project execution in an environment that integrates the project and the business

There is no argument regarding the effectiveness of the matrix management approach, despite its shortcomings and inefficiencies. However, in smaller and more agile companies, if the inefficiencies start to outweigh the benefits, then it's time to consider transitioning from strict matrix management to more of a project-based approach.

Summary

❑ Classic PM treats projects as distinct entities with well-defined and mostly static boundaries.

❑ Agile PM views projects as a core part of the business, whose boundaries are dynamic and shift with the business needs.

❑ Integrating projects into the business requires developing the organizational and project management capabilities that enable the project manager to look outside of the project boundaries.

❑ Agile PM looks to integrate the project and business environments, and thus their decision-making processes.

❑ Business and project decision making are separated in the matrix management model.

❑ Matrix management integrates the projects with the organization, but not with the business objectives.

❑ Matrix management is an effective project enabler in larger companies, but it can be an impediment to smaller organizations.

❑ A project-based organizational approach that integrates business and project decision making is better suited to the agile PM environment.

4

THE CROSS-FUNCTIONAL TEAM: ORGANIZING FOR AGILITY

Most companies running projects today are set up as some variation of the matrix, where functional managers own the resources and project managers pull individuals from the appropriate functional groups to build a cross-functional project team. The assignment to a project team is usually temporary in nature and individuals return to the their functional group when the project ends or their contribution has been completed. Whether or not your organization is based on matrix management, you will probably still have to put together some type of *cross-functional* (i.e., made up of multiple skill sets and backgrounds) team to execute your project. This chapter explores some of the dynamics of the cross-functional team that support agility. These concepts are applicable to both the matrix and project-based organizational approaches to project management, although much of the discussion is around the more commonly used matrix model.

The cross-functional team is usually formed with the stated purpose of ensuring that the team gets input and/or representation from all functional areas. This is definitely a step in the right direction to facilitate project communications. However, anyone who has led or been part of a cross-functional team will tell you that there are still challenges to overcome. Two common questions are, "Who's really leading the team?" and "What am I supposed to do?"

Who's Really Leading the Team, Anyway?

Project leadership is a sensitive topic and usually involves posturing between R&D, marketing, possibly another functional area, and the project manager. Certainly for technology companies, R&D is critical to business success. In fact, many technology companies are centered on R&D, so it seems logical that the R&D team leader should become the project leader. Then there's the marketing team leader. This person represents the customer, and it makes sense that the customer's needs should be driving the project. And finally, there's the project manager who has been *assigned* to manage the project. It's equally logical that he should be the leader.

Before going further, you need to recognize that there is both *official* and *unofficial* project leadership. The official leader is easy. That's the assigned project manager. His name goes on the organization chart and that's that. However, if another team member feels that she should really be leading the project, she could jockey to become the unofficial leader. If this individual has the organizational clout, a strong enough personality, and the support of her functional manager, she can achieve the status of unofficial project leader, thus pushing the project manager into an administrative support role. This is a real scenario that I've seen many times.

Ambiguity around project leadership is a detriment to project agility. Not only does the situation confuse the decision-making process, it creates an inefficient use of valuable resources and causes frustration in team members. Identifying this situation and resolving it as early as possible in the project will greatly increase your agility. In the uncertain and accelerated project environment, you will encounter many decision points. Approaching them in an organized and professional manner will be critical to success.

Agile Strategy

Eliminate ambiguity around project leadership by clearly defining and communicating the leadership-specific components of the key team members' roles and responsibilities (i.e., those related to running meetings, reporting to management, directing activities of other team members, and deciding on project course changes).

While there are numerous reasons that companies find themselves in this situation, one theme always seems to surface: confusion over what the project manager's role is. Most functional areas have very clear roles and responsibilities defined and agreed to throughout the organization. This is the result of many years of organizational evolution. Not so for the project manager role, which is still relatively new. In fact, I've seen organizations hire several project managers and then tell them to go forth and manage projects without any direction whatsoever. In the absence of any organizational consistency, the success of the project manager becomes largely dependent on personal skills. This is hardly a scalable project management model, and it is actually harmful to widespread adoption of project management methodologies because it creates confusion among team members as they move from project to project and see that all project managers do things a little differently.

Agile Strategy

Show the value added of project management to the team by defining, discussing, and gaining agreement on the roles and responsibilities of the project manager, including those that are leadership specific.

Additionally, without a clearly defined role, team members tend to make their own assumptions about the duties of the project manager. The visions usually involve someone telling them what to do and then constantly calling them up to ask if they're done yet. The project manager role is more often perceived as negative than positive.

This is another hindrance to PM agility. You will not be able to attain effective agility without the perception that project management is adding considerable value to the project.

Determining official and unofficial project leadership, including the role of the project manager, is difficult because it touches on politics, personalities, and organizational inertia. Effectively implementing these roles is even harder. There is no easy template solution. It's a complex organizational issue that must be addressed by any business striving to become more effective at project management. In Chapter 5, I discuss some ideas for defining the role of the project manager and having that role accepted and embraced in the organization.

What Am I Supposed to Do on This Team, Anyway?

As new projects get kicked off, project managers and functional managers alike agree that representatives from the involved functional areas need to participate on the project team. What is missing is an understanding of what all these functional representatives are supposed to do—or more appropriately, a *consistent* understanding of what they're supposed to do.

There are usually a few core groups and several support groups involved in projects. Core team members are likely to allocate 100 percent of their time to the project, while support team members may be only 10 percent allocated. This dynamic of teams composed of members with varying time commitments is critical to understand and can affect PM agility.

For dedicated team members, it is generally clear what their role is on the team. It is likely related to development or implementation, and they are accustomed to *project* work. These team members are looked to as leaders on the team and also tend to have more of a vested interest in the project's success, given their time and dedication to it. The danger to team agility comes when these dedicated members try to create excessive focus on their specific area of interest, giving it a false level of importance in the overall project and thus overshadowing other important areas. You can legitimately argue that it is your role to be a champion for your functional area; however, it should not be at the expense of other team members. The core team members need to learn to balance their influence on other team members between support of their individual/functional efforts and support of team agility.

It is very easy for an influential team member to fall into the trap of giving orders to other team members (who are perhaps looking for direction, anyway) on tasks that support his particular area alone. While this may indeed advance the core of the project, it potentially can have a negative effect on overall project agility if, for instance, a 20 percent allocated team member spends his limited time supporting the core member instead of his own area. It would be much more beneficial to the overall team effort and dynamics for the core team member to spend a small percentage of his time helping other support team members to get engaged, so they can better contribute to the project.

We will take a closer look at the roles of team members on the agile project later in Chapter 6, which covers the project team.

Agile Strategy

Get your whole team engaged in the project by encouraging the core team members to support the support team members.

Roles and Responsibilities

Defining clear roles and responsibilities is something that every project team should get into the habit of doing up-front, and it is especially important when agility is required. When I start working with a project team, either an existing team that I am joining or a new one starting up, I like to know what everyone's roles and responsibilities are. As a consultant, it helps me develop a "big picture" view of the situation. As a project manager, it helps me to help the team to properly define, plan, and execute the project. And as a participant, it helps me understand what I should and shouldn't be working on.

In the classic project management paradigm, roles and responsibilities are at least partially defined by your title or by which department you hail from. This works well in very structured organizations that have the luxury of time and that are working on largely familiar projects. It falls apart when urgency and uncertainty are introduced, in which case members need to contribute to and accept aid from all parts of the team. They define their roles and responsibilities by their expertise and their desire to achieve project milestones that are often of a cross-functional nature not seen before in the organization (see Figure 4-1). They understand that they have primary and secondary roles that are entwined with the rest of the team, and that others have roles entwined with theirs.

In essence, defined roles and responsibilities create boundaries that channel the efforts of the project team. I need to clarify that boundaries, in this case, are not barriers. Boundaries are permeable, flexible, and allow communications and information to cross over them. They allow and enable visibility into the workings of other areas. Boundaries can be thought of as guidelines that help keep individual team members and the whole team heading in the right direction. Barriers, on the other hand, tend to restrict information flow, communications, and visibility. Barriers are remnants of the old "need to know" project management mentality, whereas boundaries are facilitators of agility.

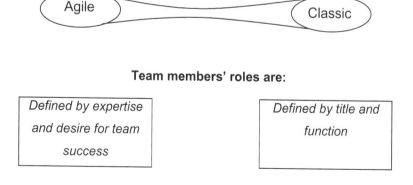

Figure 4-1. How team member roles are defined in an agile versus classic environment.

Agile Strategy

When defining the roles and responsibilities of individual team members, strive to create boundaries to guide the team, rather than barriers to restrict the team.

In an agile environment, be prepared for roles to change, be swapped, grow, shrink, and be eliminated. This is fun and it's exciting. Traditional PM defines roles and responsibilities largely to avoid turf battles. Agile PM defines them to encourage others to enter our turf (see Figure 4-2). Team members should want everyone to know what they're doing because they value their contributions. Likewise, team members should want to make their teammates successful, and it sure helps if they know what they're working on.

In the agile environment, team members need to develop the art of crossing boundaries—not because they want to be involved or share credit for parts of the project, but because diverse contributions are valuable and needed. The agile project environment is complex in nature. It requires people to stretch beyond their traditionally defined areas of expertise to solve multidimensional problems that have never presented themselves before. It used to be that if you didn't know something, then someone else usually did. In the agile environment, when you don't know something, you can't count on someone else.

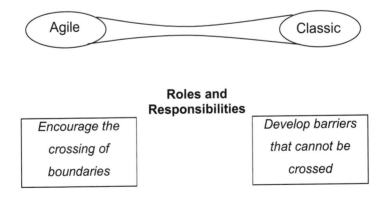

Figure 4-2. Roles and responsibilities in the agile versus classic environment.

You need to go out and figure it out, perhaps with the help of others, and then educate the team. Everyone needs to move outside his comfort zone. You will be forced to see things from new perspectives, and this is good. In this way, you will be better able to recognize seemingly unrelated events or situations spanning several areas and find ways to pull them together for the benefit of the project.

Agile Strategy

Encourage team members to cross boundaries—not to be intrusive, but to identify and create synergy among related or seemingly unrelated parts of the project.

Invariably, everyone agrees that there is great value in having clear roles and responsibilities for the project team. Yet very few teams actually spend the time to define and document them. Some teams may have a brief discussion on the topic but then forget about it. This is actually worse than doing nothing because it gives the team a false impression that there is agreement on the topic when in reality there is not. I have found that there are two primary reasons that an in-depth discussion on roles and responsibilities does not happen.

Agile Strategy

Allocate the time and energy to adequately define and discuss team roles and responsibilities. Cutting corners in this area can be worse than not doing it at all.

First, people tend to define the roles and responsibilities of their fellow teammates based on their functional area. For example, the marketing guy handles everything related to marketing, right? Well, maybe and maybe not. You may be thinking of product marketing, but the marketing guy is thinking he only handles marketing communication activities. The role of upper management and/or the project sponsor is usually quite fuzzy, too, because they haven't really given it a great deal of thought, let alone communicated their role to the working team. This situation is definitely not agile and it needs to be figured out.

Second, the definition of the term "roles and responsibilities" is often unclear and varies from person to person. Like many miscommunications, this one is often caused because people are hesitant to ask what a simple and common phrase like "roles and responsibilities" means. Agile teams will recognize this confusion and get together to hammer it out. They won't kill themselves to nail down every last detail because they know the team's dynamics may change, but they will come pretty close. Here are two simple definitions of roles and responsibilities that can be used as a starting point for discussion with your team:

❏ Your *role* defines what you *do.*

❏ Your *responsibilities* are what you *decide.* This does not include discussing information, performing analysis, or otherwise contributing information to make a decision. Responsibilities are only those areas that you regularly make decisions on for the team.

Agile Strategy

Since members of agile teams always have multiple roles, break them down into primary, secondary, and tertiary groups.

❏ Primary Role refers to something that you do *regularly* and for which you are considered the *owner* and are held *accountable* for.

❏ Secondary Role pertains to activities that you contribute to *regularly.*

❏ Tertiary Role pertains to activities that you contribute to *occasionally.*

Do not confuse your role with your time allocation. Time spent on a task does not necessarily affect your role in the project.

Agile Strategy

Break down the responsibilities of team members to avoid confusion regarding decision making in various project areas.

- ❑ Primary Responsibilities are those things that you *regularly decide* yourself. Someone else may perform analysis or make a recommendation, but you make the go/no-go decision.

- ❑ Secondary Responsibilities are those things for which you are the technical/business leader and primary *recommender,* but where someone else makes the ultimate decision.

- ❑ Tertiary Responsibilities are those things for which you are on the *committee* making the recommendation.

Decision making can fall into many categories that often interact with each other, so it's important to think through decisions critically. Common categories include business decisions, technical decisions, administrative decisions, and strategic decisions. It is also a good idea to define decision making at the milestone level, since it is here that many critical elements come together. Agile teams will find that decision making is spread more or less evenly throughout the team and mostly coincides with their primary roles. In general, the agile team will want to push decision making down to the lowest logical level, to avoid decision bottlenecks at the executive management level. Old-style teams will find decision making consolidated into a few higher-level managers where almost everyone, including the project manager, is a recommender. Decisions must be pushed up through the hierarchy before anything substantial is decided (see Figure 4-3). Obviously, this is not the most agile approach.

The primary reason that classic PM tends to push decision making up through management is that the project team usually does not have the information to make informed higher-level project decisions. As discussed in Chapter 3, making the project the business is a way for the project manager and project team to gain a higher-level perspective so that they are better able to make these decisions. In all likelihood, truly critical decisions will still be brought to senior management. However, even if intermediate-level decisions can be handled at the

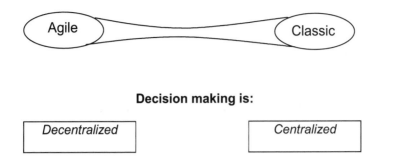

Figure 4-3. Decision making in an agile versus classic environment.

project team level, it will reduce management bottlenecks and increase agility.

Agile Strategy

Handle intermediate-level decisions at the project team level to increase agility. These are the decisions that fall in the gray area between the project team and management, thus usually making for longer and repetitive discussions leading to an actual decision.

As you've guessed by now, when defining the team's roles and responsibilities, you very well may have to define them for certain areas of management as well, since almost by definition managers are involved in decision making. Having this discussion with management can be a valuable exercise. Most agile managers want to push decision making downstream, but they may be uncomfortable in doing so. Nonetheless, the project manager and his team will take a powerful step toward agility if they can convince management to let go of some decision-making authority.

Agile Strategy

Discuss the project decision-making strategy directly with management to get their buy-in and make them comfortable with the idea of letting go of some authority.

Escalations

The process of resolving conflicts around decisions through escalations is a subset of decision making that's worthy of additional focus. This is an area that naturally crosses functional boundaries and, as such, can greatly facilitate agility—provided the process is properly worked out during the definition and planning stages of the project, rather than during a crisis in the execution stage. Many teams prefer to focus on defining "roles" and eliminate the discussion of "responsibilities" because they feel that the two are so closely aligned. That's fine, if by the team's definition, they are indeed aligned—however, this often isn't the case. There is usually alignment when responsibilities lie cleanly within a single role or functional area, but the alignment diverges when project complexities force responsibilities to cross multiple roles or functional areas. In these situations, making a decision that rightfully falls within the purview of your responsibilities may influence other people, thus creating the potential for conflict.

For instance, making the decision to modify a product feature because of a technical obstacle may influence the ultimate market position of the modified product, the compatibility with a sister product that is under development by another division, and the overall development costs. While the technical leader should be the owner of this decision, he must realize that it involves the product manager, the technical lead from the sister product, and functional management that will have to furnish additional resources to support the modification. If these people cannot agree on the technical leader's decision or, worse, were never asked in the first place, considerable conflict may arise. Who is going to unravel this mess?

The best way for the agile team to gain traction on this subject is by defining an escalation process—namely, how the team will handle conflicts in the decision-making process. If the team does decide to document responsibilities, then the escalation process should be woven into that definition. If it decides to forgo the definition of responsibilities, then the escalation process should be defined separately for the team, perhaps in the communications plan. (A detailed communications plan template is furnished at the end of this chapter.)

Agile Strategy

Define the process for escalating conflicts on the various types of decisions your team may encounter, either as part of the team responsibilities or in a separate document.

Note: Escalations are focused on conflicts or disagreements about a decision and not the decision itself. Agile teams will want to push the core decision making down to the lowest level and reserve management involvement for conflict resolution.

Often the best escalation process resolves a conflict before it actually has to be escalated at all. To this end, the agile escalation process should include a mediation step, facilitated by a third party, before bringing the problem to management. The project manager is logically this third party and therefore should be fairly skilled in conflict resolution. In fact, conflict resolution (as part of escalation) should probably be listed as a formal role of the project manager.

Agile Strategy

Include a step in the escalation process where the project manager works with the involved parties to resolve the conflict before it is actually escalated to management.

Helping the Project Team Define Its Roles and Responsibilities

Try this exercise. Document your team's current roles and responsibilities as perceived by the individual team members themselves. Have each individual write down what they think their roles and responsibilities are. While this may seem like a straightforward exercise, you are probably going to experience some confusion and debate over what a role is and what a responsibility is. The facilitator of this exercise must have a very good understanding of the differences herself in order to help the team through this question. It is not imperative that you stick strictly to my definitions, but modifications must be defendable and consistent.

Based on your particular team's dynamics, you may decide to create these definitions as a group or one-on-one. I like to have individuals create their roles and responsibilities separately and then present them to the group for discussion because it removes the potential for groupthink. In a group atmosphere, people may feel that they need to confine their roles and responsibilities to things related directly to their functional area. In reality, though, they may see other areas where they can add value. Remember, getting people to expand beyond their usual functional area, to move outside their comfort zone, should be encouraged in an agile environment. This is an opportunity to get individuals more engaged as a team, by making them think about where they can and want to contribute.   `

Once the whole team is done with their first pass at documenting roles and responsibilities, map the individual roles and responsibilities against the complete universe of roles and responsibilities required for a successful project. If you have not already defined the complete set required for the project, this is a good time to do that. As a team, discuss the following:

❑ Are there any gaps (i.e., required roles that are not covered)?

❑ Is there any overlap of primary roles?

❑ Is there a good distribution of primary and secondary roles among team members?

❑ Is there a good distribution of primary and secondary responsibilities among the team?

❑ Is the team taking ownership for intermediate-level decisions or pushing them to management?

❑ How are escalations handled?

Identification of the right resources and well-defined roles and responsibilities can have a major impact on almost all phases of a project, because without the right expertise working on the right things, the core project plan may be developed leaving critical gaps. For example, each role or responsibility should have one primary owner, but may have several secondary or tertiary contributors. If you don't cover all the bases the potential for problems—rework, delays, overruns— should be obvious. Better yet, cover "extra" bases by anticipating the unexpected. Being agile requires team members to always be looking ahead, watching out for hazards, and surveying the horizon for their next move.

Agile Strategy

Map out the entire universe of roles and responsibilities required for the project and then ensure that there is one, and only one, primary owner for each.

Meetings

One of the first things that comes to mind when discussing cross-functional teams is meetings. Meetings are an effective project management tool, but they get bad press when they are applied improperly in fast-paced business environments. In a slower-paced, fairly predictable world, meetings may be large but infrequent. It may make sense to get the whole team and all stakeholders together to present status reports and discuss accomplishments. People want to be involved and informed, and it's politically correct to invite everyone even remotely involved with the project. In general, such meetings may be valuable but not efficient. Any given participant may only be actively involved in ten minutes of an hour meeting. Still, it may be an acceptable price to pay to maintain full involvement.

Agile Strategy

Improve meeting effectiveness by increasing the number of project meetings, but limiting their scope and narrowing the invite list to only those applicable team members.

Now let's take a look at how meetings are affected by the fast-paced and uncertain business environment. First, the frequency of meetings is proportional to the level of uncertainty. Since we've already determined that there is a higher degree of uncertainty, then it follows that, in general, we need to have *more* meetings (see Figure 4-4). This usually happens by default as part of the problem-solving process. However, in our zeal to keep everyone involved, we tend to "over invite." This leads to a situation where some participants are heavily involved (which is good) and some are hardly involved (which becomes frustrating). Meeting organizers need to narrow the invite list to key contributors, and participants need to qualify their need to be present at meetings by pushing back if they feel that they cannot gain or add value.

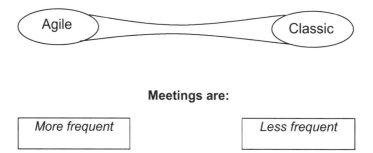

Figure 4-4. Meetings in an agile versus classic environment.

Second, project managers and team members now commonly participate in numerous projects simultaneously. It is very difficult to assess people's priorities and schedules related to projects that you are not involved in. This situation leads to meeting overload. People need the information to do their jobs but don't want more meetings. Their perception of meetings is still stuck in the past. Project managers and meeting organizers need to help shift that perception to the present. We need to be sensitive to the time demands on our resources and do everything we can to respect and support those demands. This leads me to the next point: Meetings must be run more efficiently.

Agile Strategy

Respect the time demands of team members by clearly identifying required and optional attendees at meetings. Many team members may like to remain on the distribution list and contribute when they have the time. Let them make this decision by listing them as optional attendees.

No one wants to waste time in a poorly organized and run meeting. If meetings are perceived as time-wasters, then people will stop attending, making the meeting even more inefficient for the remaining people and eventually sending the team into a downward spiral. Meeting efficiency must be emphasized in today's project teams, and while the leadership lies with the meeting organizer, the participants must also take some responsibility. Numerous books have been written on how to run good meetings, but the most important element is the agenda. You must have a good one. Enough said.

Agile Strategy

Increase meeting efficiency by sending out an agenda in advance. Include the overall meeting objectives and be clear about what you expect from attendees, so that they come prepared.

It's a "chicken or egg" situation when it comes to meetings that support project agility. We need more meetings to navigate the fast and uncertain waters, but no one wants more meetings until they can be proven to be real value-adders. A fundamental change in perceptions and culture around meetings is required for project teams to become truly agile. This is a slow process, but the first step is recognizing how changes in the project environment are reflected in our project meetings, as previously discussed.

Communications Plan

Everything discussed thus far in this chapter can be best captured in a project communications plan. The project communications plan is a document that strives to eliminate confusion by clarifying and communicating project information to both the project team and management. In addition to defining roles and responsibilities, the escalation process, and meeting protocols, the communications plan should detail how individual and team status will be tracked and reported (covered further in Chapter 10 on infrastructure) and how change notification should be handled. You may also want to include information on a team Web site, software tools that will be used for the project, including collaboration tools, and distribution methods for information. A sample template and workflow for a project communications plan is included at the end of this chapter.

Agile Strategy

Create a project communications plan to capture all elements related to decision making and communication of project information. Subsequently, exchange and discuss the communications plan with the project stakeholders.

Summary

To organize for agility, you need to assemble a cross-functional project team and establish project leadership, define the team's roles and responsibilities, and relearn how to hold effective project team meetings. Here are some key points to remember:

Cross-Functional Team Leadership

1. Team leadership can be ambiguous if not addressed directly.
2. The project manager must show his unique value-added to the team in the leadership area.
3. Core team members need to support the support team members.

Roles and Responsibilities

1. In the agile environment, roles and responsibilities are defined by expertise and desire.

2. The boundaries defined by an individual's role are permeable and should encourage others to cross those boundaries and become involved.

3. Individuals need to learn to cross boundaries in order to solve multidimensional problems that have never been encountered before.

4. Your role is what you do.

5. Your responsibility is what you decide.

6. In agile environments, decision making is decentralized.

Meetings

1. The number/frequency of meetings is proportional to the level of uncertainty. Generally, projects requiring agility will require more meetings.

2. People are generally part of several project teams simultaneously—we need to respect their limited time during meetings.

3. Meetings can be made more effective by identifying required and optional attendees, and letting them know what's expected of them so that they come prepared.

4. Project managers need to change perceptions about meetings so they can become a valuable and agile communication channel for project information.

Communications Plan Workflow

This section describes how to use the sample template when creating an actual project communications plan. It will guide you through a process that's meant to help you head off common miscommunications and facilitate the agility of your project team.

The communications plan template is designed so that individual sections can be easily included or removed from the final output. Also, there are many different types of projects, and one process definitely does not fit them all. You are encouraged to customize this process where applicable by modifying or adding sections.

An electronic copy of this workflow can be downloaded from www .xocp.com.

Identify the Project Team

Uniquely identifying the project team is a good first step toward eliminating confusion and setting project accountability.

Project Manager	This is the person responsible for managing the overall project.
Project Sponsor	This is the primary person who wants the project done and who is authorizing that resources be expended to complete it.
Team Members	These are the people who are contributing to the project. If appropriate, you may want to include a specific organization or functional area that the team member is representing on this project team.

Team Roles and Responsibilities

Clarifying the roles and responsibilities of everyone involved in the project will avoid miscommunications and confusion during project execution. Expect this section of the communications plan, more than others, to be iterative as the team works out overlaps and gaps. It is better to define roles and responsibilities in parallel or after the creation of a pro forma Project Data Sheet (see Chapter 7 on planning). These roles and responsibilities are not intended to be cast in stone, but should give the team the boundaries necessary for efficiency and agility.

Definitions:

These definitions should help get you started. You may modify them according to your team and organization needs. It is important to have a common understanding of these terms among team members.

Role: Your role is what you *do*.

Responsibility: Your responsibility is what you *decide*.

To add structure to these characteristics, you may break them down further into primary, secondary, and tertiary roles and responsibilities.

Primary Role: Something that you do *regularly* and for which you are considered the *owner* and are held *accountable* for.

Secondary Role: Things that you contribute to *regularly*.

Tertiary Role: Things that you contribute to *occasionally*.

Primary Responsibilities: Those things that you *regularly* decide yourself. Someone else may perform analysis or make a recommendation, but you make the go/no-go decision.

Secondary Responsibilities: Those things for which you are the technical/ business leader and primary *recommender,* but where someone else makes the ultimate decision.

Tertiary Responsibilities: Those things for which you are on the *committee* making the recommendation.

Review the Project Data Sheet	If you have created a Project Data Sheet (executive summary), then review it now with the team. If a Project Data Sheet has not been created yet, then review as much information about the project as is available with the team.
Agree on the definition of "roles and responsibilities"	You may use the above definitions or modify them, but it's important that everyone understands the final definitions.
Create individual roles and responsibilities	Have each individual document her roles and responsibilities. The project manager may want to facilitate this step with the project sponsor or other management that is not part of the working team.
Discuss and iterate	Review and discuss the individual roles and responsibilities with the entire team. Identify overlaps and gaps. Resolve overlaps and fill gaps.
Finalize	Based on the team discussion, finalize the roles and responsibilities for each team member. Write these in the *roles and responsibilities* section of the template.

Decisions

An up-front understanding of how decisions will be made, as well as who will make them, is critical to project agility. If all or part of this information has already been captured in the section on individual responsibilities, then it can be omitted here. Otherwise, discuss the following in the decisions section of the template.

Technical	The responsibility for technical decisions may become unclear as organizational boundaries are crossed. Clarify here if possible.
Business	Try to differentiate when a business decision can be made by the project team and when it must be brought to management outside of the project team.

Escalations

All project teams will experience conflicts and disagreements during the project. Efficiently resolving these conflicts will greatly facilitate project agility. Discuss the following in the *escalations* section of the template.

Sequence	Describe the specific sequence that escalations will take. Note if this sequence may change depending on the type of conflict.
Project team level	Describe any project team-level mediation process (led by the project manager) to attempt to resolve conflicts before escalating them to management.
Management level	Identify the specific managers that conflicts will be escalated to, depending on the type of conflict.

Practices

Practices are those behaviors, related to interacting and communicating with others, that individuals agree to observe for the benefit of their team members. Individuals should suggest practices for the team that would benefit themselves since those same practices will, more than likely, benefit others as well. The entire team should agree to the practice before documenting it here, otherwise it loses its effectiveness. Likewise, avoid practices that, while nice, are generally not realistic. For example, "everyone will show up for meetings on time" is a noble practice, but one that is rarely observed. If this was highlighted as a practice, individuals who show up on time may be agitated by those who do not. A better wording of the same practice might be "call the project manager on his cell phone if you will be more than five minutes late for a meeting."

Brainstorm and discuss practices that will prove valuable with the entire team. Write these in the *practices* section of the Communications Plan template.

General practices	Many practices are general in nature in that they can be considered common courtesy or good corporate behavior. They may already be communicated throughout the organization. An example might be the "meeting rules" that are often posted in conference rooms. There is no need to repeat these practices in the project communications plan. They should be referenced if appropriate.
	If your company has not developed any practices at the business level, then creating them initially for the project team could provide the foundation for creating company norms. In fact, developing a core group of general practices that can be leveraged across the majority of projects will prove valuable to the organization in the long run.
Project-specific practices	The most valuable practices are those that are specific to the project at hand, since these are the behaviors that may not be as obvious to the team members. For example, "SWAT team meetings will be called within four hours of receiving a level 3 customer complaint during field trials." This practice puts key players at ease, knowing that they will be kept informed of critical field trial problems.

Project Tools

Discussing and agreeing on the tools that will be used to collaborate on the project will ensure that individuals can operate efficiently as a team. It is only necessary to discuss those tools that are used to communicate or collaborate with others. For example, it is not necessary to document a statistical analysis software package that is only used by a single person and whose results are incorporated into another report for communication to the team.

Discuss and list these tools in the *project tools* section of the Communications Plan template.

Project management tools	These include the software and templates used to manage the project and communicate information about the project. Examples would be the software used to create (and read) your project timeline, progress reports, action items, or project communications plan. Everyone on the team must have access to the necessary software to contribute to the project.
Professional tools	These are tools specific to the technical characteristics of the project. Examples would be the RF test suite, laboratory protocols, and design tools/software.

| Collaboration tools | These are tools used for group collaboration and sharing of information. Examples would be a team Web site, shared drive, desktop videoconferencing, teleconferencing, online calendars, and Web collaboration space. |

Meetings

Meetings are a primary facilitator of project communication and collaboration. It is very important to set expectations with the team regarding project meetings. Without the proper forethought, meetings can become inefficient time-wasters and thus lose much of their potential value. Some meeting characteristics worthy of discussion with the team are listed below.

List the types of project meetings and their characteristics in the *meetings* section of the project Communications Plan template. It is helpful to give each regular meeting a unique name to avoid confusion.

Topic and objectives	Having meetings "just to get together" is generally inefficient and can even be frustrating for participants. All meetings should have a topic of discussion, as well as objectives describing what the meeting is trying to accomplish. Having these two characteristics defined will help keep meetings on track and greatly increase efficiency.
Frequency and duration	Understanding the frequency of regular meetings helps participants gauge what needs to be discussed at a particular meeting versus the next one. Understanding the duration helps determine the agenda and level of detail around each agenda item.
Facilitator	All meetings need a facilitator or leader to be effective. Determine who will be facilitating the meeting and what that person's responsibilities will be. The facilitator is generally the project manager, but in cases where the project manager is not an attendee, such as for a purely technical review, someone else must be designated as facilitator. Common duties of the facilitator are to create and distribute the meeting agenda and minutes. There may be other duties as well specific to the project.
Required attendees	Everyone doesn't have to be at every meeting. In fact, requiring mass attendance when it's not appropriate is a huge source of frustration among project teams. On the other hand, having a meeting where a key person is absent can be just as frustrating. Determine a list of required attendees for each meeting.
Optional attendees	Some team members may want to attend certain meetings based on their availability at a specific time and the

specific agenda topics. Other team members, and often management, like to be kept abreast of team progress by reading meeting agendas and minutes, even if they never attend. These individuals should be put on a distribution list for the meetings they may attend at their discretion.

Note: Required attendees should not be listed as optional, as this will decrease meeting effectiveness.

Individual Status Reporting

Synchronizing the many individual tasks into a cohesive project is a core value-add of project management. Likewise, repeatedly chasing down people for status reports is one of its frustrations. Avoid the aggravation associated with collecting individual status reports by agreeing up-front how reporting will be done. Status reporting can be formal or informal, and it may vary from individual to individual, depending on their particular role. Some common dimensions of individual status reporting to consider are listed below.

List how various types of status will be reported to the project manager and team in the *individual status reporting* section of the project Communications Plan template.

Type of status	Three primary project elements are of concern here: tasks (line items on the timeline), action items (activities that get assigned at meetings), and issues (problems with no immediately apparent solution). You may decide to handle these all the same way or uniquely, depending on your situation.
Audience	Determine who will receive the various status reports.
Format	The format of the status report has a great influence on project efficiency. Determine if status reports will be delivered verbally, via e-mail, or using a predefined template, an online tool, or manual markup of a printed task list, etc.
Frequency and timing	Determine how often status needs to be reported and when.

Project Status Reporting

Keeping the project sponsor and other management apprised of overall project status is also a fundamental of good project management. Some dimensions of project status reporting to consider are listed below.

List how the project's status will be reported to the project sponsor and management in the *project status reporting* section of the project Communications Plan template.

Team represen-tative	Determine who will deliver the status report. This is usually the project manager, but other core team members may need to address specific topics.
Audience	Determine who needs to receive status reports and if the same information is appropriate for all recipients.
Format	Determine the format for presenting status information. A predefined template is usually an efficient way to do this. See the Project Status Reporting workflow and template in Appendix A for a detailed example of a project reporting format.
Frequency and timing	Determine how often status needs to be reported and when.

Change Approval and Notification

Approving and communicating substantial changes to the project's scope, schedule, or resources is critical to achieving project objectives. This is even more relevant in an agile environment of frequent change. If possible, avoid having a single person or committee to approve all project changes, as this will only hinder the team's agility. Some elements to consider are listed below.

List how substantial changes to the project will be approved and communicated to the rest of the team in the *change approval and notification* section of the Communications Plan template.

Substantial	Determine some guidelines for assessing whether a particular change is "substantial" and thus warrants an official approval and notification. Minor changes should be exempt from this process.
Approvers	Determine who can approve the various types of changes.
Notification	Determine how changes will be communicated and to whom.

Template for Building a Communications Plan

(Project Name) Communications Plan

The project team:

Project manager: *name of person*

Project sponsor: *name of person*

Project team: *names of team member 1, team member 2, team member 3, . . .*

Team roles and responsibilities:

Describe the roles and responsibilities for each member of the team.

Project manager:

Project sponsor:

Team member 1:

Team member 2:

Team member n:

Decisions:

Describe how key project decisions will be made and who will make them. This section may be omitted if covered in the roles and responsibilities section.

Escalations:

Describe the process of resolving conflicts through escalation.

Practices:

Describe any organizational practices that the team agrees to observe during the project.

Project tools:

Describe any specific software or technology that will be used to manage the project and which team members should have access to it.

Meetings:

Describe the various types of meetings that will be held during the project, including meeting objectives, duration, frequency, facilitators, attendees, and any other critical characteristics.

Individual status reporting:

Describe how individual team members will keep the team informed of their progress on assigned tasks, action items, issues, etc.

Project status reporting:

Describe how the team will keep the project sponsor and other members of management informed of its progress on the overall project.

Change approval and notification:

Describe how changes to the project definition or plan will be approved and communicated to the appropriate people.

Change History

Date:	Description of change:
Today's date	As issued

5

THE PROJECT
MANAGER'S ROLE

Successfully managing projects in an agile environment is no easy task. It requires a rare combination of skills and characteristics. You will need to connect with your technical team, organize them, and drive the project forward. At the same time, you will need to allow for and guide the inevitable course changes, while keeping the project aligned with the overall business objectives. You will be challenged to balance the desire for measurable progress against the creative needs of your team and the generally iterative nature of agile PM. And you will need to do all of this while establishing and maintaining credibility with a team, where you may not be the ultimate subject matter expert. This chapter explores some of the agile PM concepts that will aid the project manager in performing these duties.

Taking an Outward Perspective

The agile project manager will take more of an outward-facing perspective versus a solely inward one (see Figure 5-1). Classic PM teaches you to focus on the project plan as your primary tool to execute and complete the project. The plan generally focuses on three key project dimensions—schedule, scope, and resource estimates—and, to

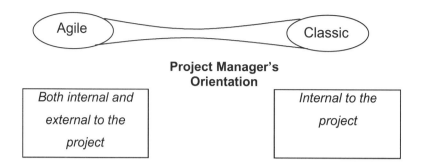

Figure 5-1. The project manager's orientation in an agile versus classic environment.

be successful, the project manager must be given some reasonable level of formal authority over the plan, as well as the project team. A common mantra is to bring the project scope in on schedule and under cost. This inward-looking perspective tends to promote a static view of the project dimensions. Since the sponsor, project manager, and team agree to a project definition and plan up-front, the perceived success or failure of the project is often based more on variation from this plan, rather than the achievement of real business objectives. If you are operating in a mature and fairly predictable project environment, then this approach works pretty well, since it emphasizes the organization and discipline necessary for success in this paradigm— when the project dimensions remain relatively stable throughout the project. However, in the uncertain environment of agile PM, we would be naïve if we did not expect changes to the project plan on several occasions, certainly much more than in a mature project environment.

Attempts to employ a strong inward-focused project management mentality in an agile environment often end up with one of three results. First, as the project progresses, it will inevitably take a few turns that were not accounted for in the original plan. If the project manager maintains an inward-facing perspective and subscribes to the notion that project performance is based on the team's ability to deliver what they signed up for (i.e., the original plan), then he will spend a good portion of his time analyzing and documenting these variations from the original plan. As the zigs start to mount where the plan called for a zag, the project manager will soon be consumed with tracking, analyzing, and documenting ever more complex variations. When this happens, the project manager reduces himself to what is essentially an administrative support role. While it is certainly smart to understand why your project is off its planned course, as project manager you need to keep your eye on accomplishing your project objective—not on excessive paperwork.

Second, if the project manager is strong enough and has solid support from management, he can develop into a dreaded taskmaster—someone who is constantly on the team members to get tasks done on time and perhaps ahead of time (if he's really aggressive). From the team-building perspective, I don't think that this ever goes over well. In extreme cases, it can end up destroying the project. From a strict, project-efficiency perspective, this approach may work in the very predictable project environment, where the tasks are fairly rote and there's not much chance for deviation from the plan. However, as in the other examples that we've discussed, this method is unlikely to be successful when iteration and multiple paths are required to reach the final destination. Project managers taking this tact in an agile environment will be showing the team that they really don't understand how to manage agile projects, which leads us to the next scenario.

Agile Strategy

Do not become a taskmaster. If tasks are not getting done, the project team probably feels that the internal project plan needs to change. Look outside of your project for nontechnical points that support or dissuade these changes, then present them to the technical leaders for discussion.

The third possibility is that the project manager simply loses credibility with the project team. The team knows that the original plan needs to shift, but the inward-focused project manager sees changes to the plan as variances that will only delay the project and impact his perception of project success. The team members may not know explicitly what the project manager needs to do (after all, it's not their job), but they do know that sticking steadfastly to the original plan isn't it. While there is certainly some room for debate, the project manager must be prepared to try some alternative approaches, or risk losing credibility. If he cannot strike a balance or justify his position with the team, passive and active resistance may develop. Eventually, the project manager risks being pushed, once again, into an administrative support role, thus greatly reducing the value that he could add to the project.

The agile project manager recognizes that changes and iterations to the plan will happen. In fact, they are necessary for the project's ultimate success. She will look for ways to help direct those changes in a way that will support the high-level business needs, rather than fighting them on the grounds of outdated project boundaries.

Agile Strategy

Continually scan the external environment, looking for business drivers that may affect the project. Identifying these influences for the team will help you make the right course changes during the project.

By scanning the environment outside of the project itself, the project manager can identify business drivers that, when combined with the technical drivers, will help the team decide which direction to go when confronted with a fork in the road. The rest of the project team is focused internally. From their internal focus, the team will drive change from a technical perspective. The project manager should balance those technical inputs with the corresponding external influences. If she doesn't do this, the project risks falling out of alignment with the business objectives.

Rather than waiting for some unexpected, external event to come crashing down on the project, the project manager should actively search the external environment for such events. Just as individuals may bring technical issues and information to the rest of the team for discussion and consideration, the project manager should bring external business information back to the team so that they can evaluate its impact on their work.

Agile Strategy

Add value to the team and gain credibility by bringing relative, external information to the table so it can be discussed along with the technical elements surfaced by other team members.

If the project manager is not a technical expert, it is even more important to look outward for valuable information that may affect the project. In an agile environment, the project manager is rarely handed formal authority over the team. She must establish her own credibility to successfully lead the team. In this situation, a surefire way to lose credibility is for the project manager to challenge technical experts on technical issues. On the other hand, a way to gain credibility is to trust that team members know what they're doing, while bringing them additional, valuable information from outside of the project that complements their own information.

You may ask, "With all this looking outside the project, who's watching the plan?" The answer is: You are. It's just that you'll spend less energy focused on driving the original plan and more energy on facilitating the changes that will get you to your final destination. I realize that there are only so many hours in the day. Surveying the external environment, in addition to watching the internals of the project, may be overload. This leads me into the discussion of the agile project management infrastructure, which is a topic discussed in further detail in Chapter 10. In essence, an agile PM infrastructure is a concise toolkit geared toward efficiently managing the relevant internals of project execution, thus freeing up much of the project manager's time to focus externally.

Tracking External Trends and Variances

An interesting dynamic of having an external view is that, when it expands your perspective of the project, it leads you to monitor untraditional metrics as barometers of project progress. In classic PM, the project manager usually monitors variance to the internal elements of schedule, scope, and cost to judge project success. However, in an agile project, monitoring variance to the plan may be a futile exercise. As project managers, we want to facilitate the correct course changes necessary for project success. Making the actual course-change decisions is probably driven by both technical needs and external events, and you must consider both. Since these decisions are influenced by external events, you'll need to monitor variances and trends in these events (see Figure 5-2).

By monitoring the trends in external business influencers, the project manager and team are better able to make the decisions that will keep their project aligned with the true business needs. It is in these tactical project decisions that the integration of the project and the business really pays off.

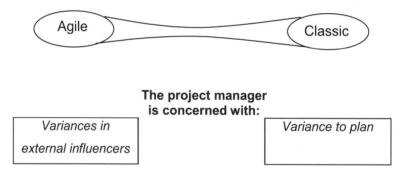

Figure 5-2. Trends and variances monitored by the project manager in an agile versus classic environment.

Agile Strategy

Track trends of key external influencers, as well as variances from what is expected, and you will move from being reactive to proactive.

The Project Manager as Facilitator and Leader

In the agile environment, the project manager is more of a facilitator than a manager. She must rely on her influencing skills, rather than on formal authority, to get things done. Oftentimes, she (the project manager) is a peer to the individual team members in the organizational pecking order. Acting as a facilitator is nonthreatening to peers, whereas acting as a *manager* (i.e., giving orders) can be perceived as overstepping her bounds, making it more difficult to establish herself with the team. As her credibility is established, the project manager may evolve into a coach and sounding board for second opinions. Once this happens, the team will be discussing technical obstacles with the project manager instead of withholding them from the taskmaster. As the project manager increasingly becomes the melting pot for project information (both internal and external), she may soon find herself in the enviable position of project leader.

Agile Strategy

Act as more of a facilitator than a manager. Not only is this approach nonthreatening and less confrontational, it will help you establish yourself with the team so that you evolve into its leader.

The road to establishing leadership in an agile environment is a tricky one. Rarely will the project manager have formal authority over the project team. She may have the "project manager" title bestowed upon her, but like other individual contributors on the team, she must prove her worth. The key difference between the project manager and other individual contributors is that there is an implicit assumption that the project manager role is that of a leader. So, while it is relatively straightforward to prove your worth in a technical role, this isn't the case when trying to prove your worth in a leadership role. When you're working in an innovative environment filled with top performers, ideas, and energy, the ability to facilitate the distillation and analysis of large amounts of information into a usable form that everyone can agree on is extremely valuable. Once you show the team that you can help them make sense out of chaos, you will be taking a large step toward becoming the team leader.

Agile Strategy

Distill the reams of technical and business project data into usable information. You will not only add immense value, but you will also gain credibility with the team by performing a difficult task that doesn't clearly fall under anyone else's domain.

Alignment and Channeling

Despite a lack of formal authority, the agile project manager must still be able to direct the project and the team. There are still some necessary aspects of the classic, planning-and-control line of attack, but the agile project manager must take a softer approach (see Figure 5-3). Instead of driving compliance to a potentially outdated plan, she must keep the project aligned with the changing project environment. The agile project manager is like an information manifold that takes in technical and business information from many sources, organizes and reconciles it, and then channels it to the appropriate team members and sponsors. I've heard many project managers lament that they wish they were making more technical contributions to the project. This is a noble thought, but rather than spending time trying to make technical contributions, or reverting back to the classic project management control methods, you should be tuning up your manifold. The constant change involved in an agile project requires an information manifold that is constantly pulling in new information, digesting it, analyzing it, and distributing it to the right people. This is perhaps the single most valuable contribution an agile project manager can make during the execution phase of a project.

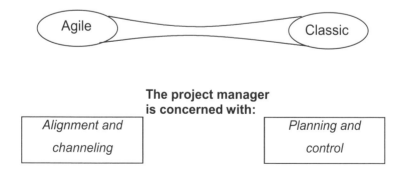

Figure 5-3. The project manager's focus in an agile versus classic environment.

Agile Strategy

Act as an information manifold to efficiently distribute the distilled information to the appropriate team members. This highly valuable role provides a key linkage between the project and its external environment, and it puts you out in front of both the project team and sponsors.

Perhaps manifold is not the perfect analogy, since it implies a rote and simplistic method of distribution. This is probably true in a repeatable environment, but not so in the agile one. Here, you need to be an intelligent manifold (see Figure 5-4). When you are in the midst of a dynamic technical and business environment, knowing which events are important to the project (and which are not important) is critical to making the correct decisions. Knowing where to look for the information, and then getting it, can be challenging. Reconciling the constant flow of information against your (agile) plan takes effort. Analyzing various "what if" scenarios is a skill to be honed. And finally, packaging the information and channeling it to the right people at the right time is key to success. By acting as an *intelligent* information manifold, you do two things. First, you establish credibility with the technical team by adding value where there was none before. And second, you influence the direction of the project by channeling the appropriate information to the appropriate decision makers, at the ap-

Internal & External Information

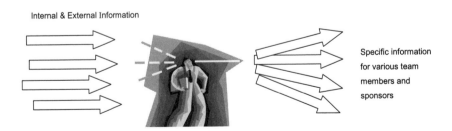

Specific information for various team members and sponsors

Figure 5-4. The project manager acts as an intelligent information manifold to distribute key project information to team members and sponsors.

propriate times. An outline of the mechanical parts of the manifold is also discussed in Chapter 10.

Building Relationships with Key Stakeholders

There are people outside of the project team who are core participants during the definition and planning stages, but who are often fringe players during the execution stage. These stakeholders include the project's end customers, other project managers, functional management, and executive management. While we may strive for a fully integrated and project-based organization where the project manager and team are bestowed with substantial decision-making authority, in most cases, this just isn't reality. In these situations, critical decisions will have to be signed off by the appropriate stakeholders. It is not enough to merely keep these people "in the loop." You will need to have a previously established *relationship* to facilitate the difficult decision making that needs to happen in the heat of the moment. Presenting the facts is definitely a project management duty, but having preestablished credibility and trust will go much further than just facts when trying to a get approval for an urgent and critical action. When you go to an executive with a crucial recommendation you want to hear her say, "Listen, Anne, it doesn't seem like we have the time to revisit all the facts. I trust your judgment; just make it happen." That's also an incredible morale and energy booster!

Agile Strategy

Find time to spend with key stakeholders when the project is going smoothly, so that when a crisis hits you will have already built a solid relationship in which you are trusted to make the correct decisions under fire.

Building a relationship of professional trust requires work and time. By *work,* I mean that it's not just fluff and shooting the breeze. You need to initiate professional discussions on substantial topics so that you can demonstrate your ability to identify, analyze, and present the most valuable nuggets of information to that particular stakeholder. By *time,* I mean that you simply cannot rush your relationship-building duties; you must plan for them. An executive has time for only those nuggets of information that are truly valuable, and these may come along once a month or less. Your task is to *consistently* pick up these nuggets before their value wanes, while filtering out the junk. The key is to spend time early on with your stakeholders so they can describe to you, as precisely as possible, what their particular nuggets looks like. One last point: If you're not finding any nuggets, be patient. If you get overanxious and try to use junk information to build your relationship, you'll more than likely lose credibility faster than if you did nothing at all.

Agile Strategy
Build credibility with stakeholders by working with them to learn how to recognize their critical few (gold) nuggets. Then, patiently and consistently, extract the real nuggets for them while filtering out the junk.

Filling the Gaps

Another way that project managers can add value in the agile environment is through filling gaps. Agile projects are often trying to do something that has never been done before, so it is reasonable to expect that gaps or holes in the project plan will appear as the project progresses. Furthermore, many of these gaps will not fall cleanly under the responsibility of any given team member. Likely locations for cracks to form are where the technical aspects of the project meet the business elements, or where there are handoffs between different functional areas. This is a perfect opportunity for the project manager to jump in and help bridge a gap that could otherwise become a stumbling block for the team. Not only is this a way to add real value to the project, thus helping to establish credibility, it's a way for the proj-

ect manager to get more deeply integrated with the technical side of
the project without stepping on anyone's toes.

Agile Strategy

Look for ways to fill gaps in the project plan or that have formed
during project execution. You can fill these gaps yourself or by finding
additional resources. Either way, you will not only be adding value,
but you will be brought deeper into the fold by the technical team.

Managing the Interactivity

Project managers are in the unique position of being involved in all
key aspects of the project. They don't necessarily approve or even
have a say in many critical decisions, but they have the opportunity to
observe these events and the overall decision-making process. An agile
project manager will take advantage of this inimitable perspective to
advance his project by raising the level of effective activity and interactivity among team members.

In a dynamic environment, individuals can lose sight of the really
important tasks, especially when they are not privy to the entire picture. I've seen projects where one part will come to a complete stop,
while another is frantic with activity. And I've seen other projects
where everyone wants to work on the same set of activities, while
there are numerous other things that need to be attended to. Or, there
are other projects where subparts of the project are duplicated because
team members don't know what other team members are doing. All
of these cases are examples of energetic and dedicated people trying
their best to advance their project as fast as possible, but without complete information or involvement. In a stable project environment, or
in the initial project planning, this is not a problem. It only becomes
a challenge in the dynamics of the project execution. This is when the
project manager must step forward and direct traffic for the team. No
matter how little technical contribution the project manager may be
making, he knows what is being worked on and by whom, thus put-

ting him in the best position to bring people together, inform sub-teams of relevant developments, and fill the gaps in order to ensure success.

Agile Strategy

When the project becomes dynamic during the execution stage, your first action should be to facilitate the activities and interactivity of team members to support project and business objectives, before updating the detailed plan.

Managing the Plan

The agile project manager cannot lose sight of his project plan, but he also doesn't have to obsess over it. We know that the plan is in a near-constant state of change and that it needs to be maintained, but we also know that that's not our number-one priority. If we devote the bulk of our time to chasing the changing plan, we diminish our value to the team and will be (subconsciously) reverting to classic PM techniques in an agile environment. In the classic paradigm, control is very important for the project manager, and, in order to have control, you need a solid plan—thus the need to maintain an up-to-date plan. In the agile project, we spend more energy on information absorption and analysis, rather than constantly updating the plan.

In managing the plan for the agile project, the project manager needs to rely heavily on her facilitation and information manifold skills. Technical team members are often experts in a fairly small area, and they do not always see the bigger picture. This doesn't mean that they are not interested in the overall project, just that they may not have the bandwidth to stay abreast of everything in the project while still driving the part that they own. In fact, when presented with the "big picture" implications of various project alternatives, I've found that most technical people can readily assimilate the information and provide thoughtful feedback. These team members want to understand the entire scope of the project because it puts the project in a business perspective, and it enables them to understand the complexity and value of making the project successful. It is also helps them prepare for the inevitable course changes in the project down the road, because they always have the overall picture in the back of their heads.

Agile Strategy

Maintain a "big picture" view of the whole project (the technical and business sides) and keep it in front of the team. This provides a medium for soliciting high-level input from team members, as well as the opportunity for encouraging deeper engagement by individuals because they can see how their contributions fit into the larger picture.

One of the more frustrating project management duties is collecting the information necessary to track progress against the plan. This basically involves determining whether tasks have been completed as planned or are on track to be completed as planned, and if not, why and what is being done about it. In most cases, team members do not voluntarily come forward to report their individual status to the project manager. This results in one or both of the following scenarios. First, the project manager must follow up with each individual and ask about the status of their tasks. This never seems to be very comfortable, especially when tasks are behind schedule, and it certainly is not efficient for the project manager. Second, the project manager can call a meeting with the whole team at once, to review the status of all open tasks. This is more efficient for the project manager but highly inefficient for the team members. Valuable time during team meetings should be reserved for critical discussion, analysis, and brainstorming that can benefit from the synergy of the whole team and not be wasted on mundane status collection activities. This seemingly basic project management activity can seriously bog down a project if not handled properly. Creating a status collection process during the project definition stage, discussing it with the team, and including it in the project communications plan will go a long way toward increasing agility.

Agile Strategy

Define, discuss, and gain up-front agreement on a mechanism/practice that sets expectations regarding how and when individuals will report on the status of their tasks. You'll gain across-the-board efficiency during project execution as a result.

Lessons Learned

It goes without saying that mistakes will be made when operating in an uncertain environment. The trick, of course, is to learn as much as possible from each misstep, adding to the knowledge base of the organization and, hopefully, not making the same mistake again. There are three parts to the basic lessons learned process. First, develop an environment that supports continual learning. Second, capture key lessons learned. And third, archive, organize, and make these learnings accessible to current and future project teams.

Many organizations believe that they are too busy to spend time looking back. They think it's a waste of time, or worse, they are embarrassed to bring attention to poor behavior, decisions, or performance. Breaking this type of culture will go a long way toward improving both short-term and long-term success in the agile environment. The agile project operates in an atmosphere of high interactivity, boundary crossing, and multiple simultaneous pathways. Team members need to have conviction in their opinions, be able to consider alternative viewpoints, and come to agreeable conclusions among themselves. In a nutshell, they need to be able to work effectively together. While this is the case in almost all of business, it is emphasized here because of the higher levels of interaction among team members who, perhaps, are not used to working together. By inserting lessons learned sessions (either periodically or at major milestones) into your overall project plan, you will be putting the team on notice that their actions will be reviewed and captured. When organizations first start this process, it tends to gravitate toward team dynamics, both positive and negative, as the team learns how to work together in the agile paradigm. Once the interpersonal dynamics are worked out, the lessons learned tend to shift toward technical and business decision making, but by this time your team will be well on its way to becoming truly effective in the agile environment.

Agile Strategy

Support and allocate time for a consistent "lessons learned" process. By creating an environment of intrateam- and self-accountability, you will accelerate the development of effective working relationships among your team members.

Effectively and efficiently capturing the lessons learned from your projects is the key enabler to making this process successful. There are numerous ways to perform this process, but key elements are that it must be easy to use, take minimal time, have full involvement, and provide fast feedback to the participants. Without at least touching on these areas, the process can become too drawn out and analytic for the agile project, thus stalling its progression, rather than accelerating it. The goals should be to quickly capture what went well and what could be improved. There should be a brief discussion on the results, and then the team should move on. Some action items may be assigned as an output from the process, but they should not hinder forward progress of the overall project or the next project. If you already have a lessons learned process, take a look at it from the agile perspective and consider the aforementioned points. As a target, try to limit team involvement in the process to one to two hours total. If you go over two hours, the process will get too heavy for the agile environment, and you'll need to make some modifications. If you don't currently have a formal process, an example is included at the end of this chapter that can be used as a starting point for you to customize to your project environment.

Finally, archiving, organizing, and communicating your lessons learned will be a foundation of your long-term success. Certainly, results should be immediately communicated to the participants via e-mail or other project communication. However, teams should be able to learn from the lessons of other teams as well as their own. Creating some type of online and organized archive system is the best way to do this. Knowledge management is a relatively sophisticated topic unto itself and is not discussed here, however, I discuss the basics of a manual project management infrastructure that would cover the long-term archiving and accessibility of lessons learned in Chapter 10.

Interpersonal Skills

The successful agile project manager must balance the freedom required by highly creative teams with classic PM duties such as schedule tracking and progress reporting in order to drive the project forward. Solid interpersonal skills are essential to managing in the agile environment. A heavy-handed approach is rarely successful. The trick is to let the team run as free as possible, while maintaining the ability to pull them back in when necessary. However, relying solely on soft skills may not always be enough to pull off this critical balancing act. In addition to employing superior interpersonal skills, the project manager can play the roles and use the processes described in this chapter to stay on top of the project *and* establish the credibility with the team necessary to effectively lead it through the storm of uncertainty—and do it all without stepping on anyone's toes.

Summary

The agile project manager's role combines many duties and skills. The agile project manager:

- ❏ Recognizes that agile projects will change direction often through the course of the project
- ❏ Takes an outward-facing perspective to scan the external environment for influences that will affect the project, subsequently bringing these elements back to the project team

❏ Is more of a facilitator than a manager

❏ Acts as an intelligent information manifold

❏ Proactively works to build relationships with project stakeholders during the calm times of the project

❏ Uses "gap filling" as a means to add value and become more integrated in technical projects

❏ Maintains a "big picture" view of the project for the team

❏ Facilitates the activities and interactivities of individual team members

❏ Champions the development of organizational project knowledge through the lessons learned process

❏ Combines solid interpersonal skills, a light-handed approach, and the roles described in this chapter to effectively drive the project forward

The Lessons Learned Process (aka the Retrospective or Sunset Review)

Emerging and agile organizations developing new project management tools and processes will inevitably go through some iteration as the new PM processes are tuned to their project and business environment. The fast pace of the agile environment often encourages us to forget mistakes and just move on. While this approach is probably more efficient at solving the immediate problem at hand, it is generally detrimental to the long-term optimization of the organization's PM infrastructure, as well as its ability to effectively define, plan, and execute projects. The process described here is designed to be a "light" process that can be easily and frequently applied to capture the lessons learned from our most recent events and projects. An electronic copy of this process can be downloaded from www.xocp.com.

Introduction

Purpose	The purpose of the Lessons Learned process is to capture best practices and improvement areas upon the completion of a project, major milestone, or substantial event, so that problems can be addressed and successes repeated in the future.
Overview	This process has three parts. The first part is a brainstorming session, the second is a silent reorganization, and the third is a group discussion.
Preparation	In preparation, each participant should think of several specific things about the project that: 1. Could be improved 2. Went well
Timing	It is best to use the Lessons Learned process relatively soon after the completion of the project milestone or event, so that participants still have it fresh in their minds.
Time	Expect this process to take between one-half hour and two hours, depending on the project size, the number of participants, and the complexity. With some experience, you will be able to judge the time required based on the amount of material to be covered. In turn, you should space the Lessons Learned sessions so that the target time allocation for this process is approximately one hour.
Roles	There is one facilitator, one scribe, and several participants. The facilitator leads the team through the process. He/she should be as unbiased as possible, which means the facilitator is often not part of the project team (how-

	ever, this is not a requirement). The scribe captures team comments that don't get written down during the exercise for inclusion in the write-up. Participants may include any team member or stakeholder of the project.
Setting	This exercise is best performed in a conference room with a table and plenty of wall space or a whiteboard.
Supplies	Easel paper, large Post-It notes, markers, and tape.
Setup	Tape several pieces of easel paper together, and then tape them up on the wall in the conference room. Label them "What could be improved?" Tape together several more sheets of easel paper on another wall and label them "What went well?"

Process

Participant guidelines	Focus on the process and not on the people. Anything related to the project is fair game. No judgment should be passed on other people's ideas. Only the participant presenting his/her idea should be speaking.
Facilitator guidelines	Remain unbiased. Try to get equal participation from the group. Do not let any individual or small group dominate the exercise. The facilitator can participate (if he/she so desires), but should be conscious to not lead the group in any particular direction. Help the group follow the process below.

What Could Be Improved?

Overview	These next two sections are where the brainstorming takes place. The idea is to get as many ideas on the table as possible. They do not have to be mainstream or hot ideas; in fact, it's often the corner or edge cases that add the most long-term value since they are often overlooked.
Step 1	The facilitator asks the participants to write their top three to five "What could be improved?" ideas on Post-It notes (one idea per note). This should be done individually and without discussion.
Step 2	When the participants are done, the facilitator selects a random participant and puts her note up on the "What could be improved?" easel paper. The notes can be placed anywhere on the easel paper.

Step 3	When selected, the participant describes her idea/suggestion to the group. Other participants should not make comments agreeing or disagreeing with the idea being presented. Only questions of clarification may be asked.
Step 4	The facilitator then selects the next participant to present his idea. This goes on until all participants have presented one idea.
Step 5	Once everyone has presented one idea, the facilitator starts around the room again. This goes on until all ideas have been presented. *Note:* Ideas may start to be repeated, and this is okay. The discussion can be abbreviated.

What Went Well?

Overview	This section is the same as the previous one, except that it asks the question, "What went well?" For this process, the facilitator and participants repeat the steps 1–5 in the previous section to collect and brainstorm their ideas.

Silent Reorganization

Overview	There are probably numerous ideas on each side now. Many of the ideas are related, or only have minor differences. The intent of this section is to group the ideas into major themes. This is done in silence to prevent one or a few individuals from dominating/influencing the groupings.
Step 1	The facilitator invites half of the team to approach the "What could be improved?" idea set and the other half the "What went well?" idea set. The participants are instructed to move the notes into related groups. Anyone can move any note, including ones that have been moved by other participants. It is normal to see the same note moved several times back and forth by different members of the group. The catch is that there can be no talking during this part of the exercise.
Step 2	The participants should move between "What could be improved?" and "What went well?" so that they have the chance to work on both sets of ideas.
Step 3	If there appears to be a conflict about the placement of any particular note that cannot be resolved silently, the

	facilitator may duplicate the note and, thus, place it in multiple spots.
Step 4	Continue this process until the movement of notes stops.

Discussion

Overview	The facilitator leads the discussion on each of the major themes that emerged from the previous step.
Step 1	A heading should be agreed to by the team and added to each grouping of notes. The facilitator should also ask if there were any other themes/groupings that people noted but that got reorganized out. These should be captured now by adding the heading to the appropriate easel paper.
Step 2	New comments, suggestions, and ideas should be captured on a new note and added to the appropriate group.
Step 3	Once all of the groups of notes have been discussed, the facilitator should summarize the findings, identify any action items, and thank the team for participating.
Step 4	The facilitator should write up the results from the scribe's notes and the easel paper, being sure not to move anything from its final resting point. (It's a good idea to tape down the notes before taking down the easel paper.) There is not any editorializing done here. Simply capture the major themes, as well as the Post-It note comments under each one. Action items should be transferred to the team's active "action item" list for follow up.
Step 5	Publish the results of Lessons Learned to the whole team, including the members that didn't, or couldn't, participate. Archive the results and make them accessible for future review.

6

THE AGILE PROJECT TEAM

A project team that "gels" can be a joy to work on. A cohesive team is, very possibly, the key between success and failure in the agile environment. Most of us have had the good fortune to have been part of such a team at least once in our careers, but we probably have many more stories of mediocre and even dysfunctional teams. Numerous dynamics may combine to make a team "click." This chapter is not about overall team dynamics; rather, it explores some of those characteristics common to the successful agile project team. If you are selecting your next team, then this chapter should give you some ideas about what to look for in your members. If you're already part of a team, this chapter may give you some ideas to make your team more agile.

Common Skills

The so-called soft skills are a critical common denominator of agile team members. These skills include the ability to create and maintain relationships, interact with various levels and functions within the organization, flexibility, adaptability, and generally being a team player.

These traits are commonly referred to in most discussions on team dynamics and, indeed, they are invaluable to any team.

In the agile environment, the value of solid interpersonal skills is amplified. Agile projects tend to pursue multiple simultaneous pathways. The agile team needs to be able to operate within and evolve this network of pathways to advance the overall project. The networked nature of the agile project team requires the average team member to interact directly with many more people in the organization than may be necessary in the classic environment, where members have well-defined and compartmentalized roles.

Broad technical skills are also a must for the agile team. This may seem obvious, but again, the need for technical know-how is somewhat amplified in the agile environment. To maintain their responsiveness, agile teams are generally smaller. Fewer people per team means team members must be able to wear multiple hats. All relevant areas of expertise for the project must be covered, but there isn't room for much overlap. If you're responsible for a certain functional contribution to the team, then you must be able to carry the ball in that area. Others are available to collaborate with you, but you must be able to make the final determination. In other words, it is difficult for a rank novice, who is still learning on the job, to play a core role on an agile team.

Agile Strategy

Discourage everyone from wanting to work on the high-visibility tasks, because that creates internal competition. Instead, show there's value in contributing to other areas of the project. You can do this by painting the "big picture" and carefully defining team member roles and responsibilities.

This does not mean that you should assemble the top experts across your organization for an agile team. In fact, that may be detrimental. Too many experts may create unhealthy tension in the form of posturing for leadership or high-visibility tasks, excessive debate, and one-upsmanship. When this happens, the project manager must address the situation quickly before the team dynamics start to spiral downward. As discussed in Chapter 5 on the role of the project manager, creating well-defined roles and responsibilities is a good tactic for mitigating this problem. On the other hand, while the agile team is not necessarily a good place for someone with novice-level skills and experience, it is a great place for someone with intermediate-level skills. Today's businesses require well-balanced team members in all areas. The agile team, being on one extreme of the spectrum, is a great training ground for the person who has mastered a specific functional skill and is ready for exposure to other functional areas. Certainly, experts are required on the team in the core technical and business areas, but mixing people with intermediate-level skills into the support areas of the team tends to create a good balance.

Agile Strategy

Select a mix of expert and intermediate-level skill sets to create a healthy balance on the team, and provide a training ground for broadening individual perspectives.

Uncommon Skills

The soft skills required in an agile team member go beyond just being able to get along with people, being a team player, and participating in a network. Individuals on the agile team must be able to *initiate* the networks that make up the agile project. They actively seek out others for collaboration and information. They help other team members become engaged when they are in a rut. They go out of their way to offer their services and assistance to others. They create a barrage of ideas to investigate rather than focusing on just one. And their strong interpersonal skills enable them to do all of this in a positive light.

**Very few people have the uncommon skill
to be able to create the networks of ideas
and people necessary to drive innovative
projects forward.**

Many of the problems of uncertainty encountered in agile projects are addressed by exploring multiple simultaneous pathways versus the single path common in classic project management. Being able to generate and then link various idea networks is crucial. This lays out the team's options before them, facilitating decision making in the face of the unexpected. More than the actual ideas themselves, the people who brainstorm these ideas, and subsequently commit to executing them, become part of the project network. Often the individuals who get pulled into the network of an agile project are not even formally part of the team, yet they make significant intellectual contributions to its success. Many people have the skills to join and contribute to a network. Very few people have the uncommon skill to be able to create one. Certainly, not everyone on an agile project team needs to be a network creator, but at least someone must assume that role. It could be the project manager or the technical leader, but ideally, someone on the core team. You may find that no one is instinctively adept at this skill. That's okay, as long as you recognize it. In that case, the key players on the team must put additional conscious effort into the network creation process.

Agile Strategy

Look outside of your specific technical area to identify where your efforts intersect those of other team members, as well as those who are not even part of the current project plan. In this way, you will be creating a network of ideas that will help drive your ideas forward.

Throughout this book, I have discussed the effect of operating a project in an uncertain environment—specifically, an environment where the project requirements are expected to change many times over the project's duration. The project will most likely change schedule and scope multiple times, but it may also change team members, roles of team members, sponsors, and leadership. These resource-related changes often originate within the project and, in turn, force the surrounding organization itself to change.

Being able to manage a project through uncertain territory is a challenge in itself, but dealing with the effects of organizational change surrounding the project is quite a different thing altogether. A common occurrence on an agile team that affects the surrounding organization is when team members move outside of their traditional roles. I like to encourage this behavior on the agile team; however, individuals who don't subscribe to this philosophy will inherently resist and perhaps pull their functional management into the project realm to protest. This happens when their functional management has erected solid barriers around their territory and instilled in people the idea that they shouldn't be working outside the barrier and others shouldn't be working inside it. When people move outside their traditional roles, it may cause organizational conflict because it appears to be a prelude to organizational change—which, in a way, it is. So, in addition to being a methodology for managing projects in an uncertain environment, agile project management is an influence on organizational culture to break down the so-called silo mentality.

Agile Strategy

Break down the silo mentality by presenting the big picture of the project, depicting the networked pathways to functional management. Explain to them why functional boundaries need to be crossed.

Let's take a step back and clarify that we are now talking about *organizational* change, where previously we were discussing *project* change. Project change is something that we have to deal with because we are breaking new ground and we don't have a template or map to lead us. Organizational change is something that we must *drive,* if necessary, to make the agile project successful. If your business is running a project in an environment of uncertainty, then the business itself is in the same environment. The project will undoubtedly change directions on its way to completion, and the organization may very well have to change with it. This can be scary for some people, but remember, the project is the business (Chapter 3's lesson). It is very difficult to move the project forward if the organization is stalled.

The agile team must be able to deal with changes in the project and must be able to *drive* changes in the organization.

You want people on the team who not only can tolerate change, but also thrive on change. Ideally, you'll find individuals for your team with that very uncommon skill of being able to drive organizational change. Let's call them organizational architects. This reinvention may be at the department or the division level or somewhere in between. The agile team is not afraid to challenge the organization to transform itself, especially when the transformation is necessary to stay competitive in the changing business environment.

Agile Strategy

Add an organizational element to the project plan describing the benefits of new organizational roles and responsibilities, both to stimulate team discussion and provide a basis for discussion with management.

These organizational architects can visualize the impact of the shifting business environment and craft new ways for the organization to adapt. Furthermore, they can communicate their vision to decision makers in management (since they usually do not hold formal authority to dictate an organizational change) and convince management to take action. While many people are skilled at incrementally improving business processes, few are skilled at crafting improved organizations. I've seen many job advertisements for business process analysts, reengineering experts, or process engineers, but never one for an organizational architect. Yet you want people with these skills on your team. These people know that having an agile project team is only part of the battle. It doesn't matter how agile the team is if it is continually being weighed down by a business organization that's incapable of changing. To complement an agile team, you need agility in the overall business. Creating organizational agility will be paramount to business survival in the future. Driving this change from the project perspective is a very effective means, since projects are the vehicles dealing with current real-world scenarios.

Working Together, Working Alone

Individuals on the agile team must be able to thrive in environments of both collaboration and solitude. They are self-starters who can assess the situation and determine for themselves which work mode they should be in, and then get themselves (and perhaps other team members) into it. As the project progresses through its lifecycle, the need for individuals to be working together or working alone will flip-flop many times. In some cases, team members may be working on parallel tasks and have to work in both modes simultaneously. The uncertain nature of the agile project creates this flip-flop between the optimized work mode (collaboration or solitude) and places a higher emphasis on the team's ability to efficiently switch between modes. This concept is similar to trying to determine how many different projects one person can effectively contribute to simultaneously. There are inherent "switching" inefficiencies as a person transitions from one project to another. If you give him too many projects, the inefficiencies become greater than his effective contribution. In the agile paradigm, you may be working on a single project, but whether you work alone or with others is changing frequently. If you cannot effectively change work modalities, your switching inefficiencies will negate your contributions, essentially making you an ineffective team member.

Agile projects are more iterative than classic ones. At a high level, this means that instead of first developing a complete plan and then executing it, we may do a less detailed plan, execute, analyze, and then repeat. This cycle may recur many times during the course of the project. For example, planning is generally a collaborative effort since the agile project is made up of a network of related activities. Execution may or may not require collaboration, and the same is true for analysis. Furthermore, each collaborative step may require a different group of people getting involved. Adding this "work modality" dimension to the already numerous "task or functional" dimensions makes the agile project that much more interesting.

Agile Strategy

Find individuals who have successfully worked remotely on projects in the past. They are likely to thrive in the agile environment because they can efficiently shift between work modes.

Identifying people who can efficiently switch work modes may not be the easiest thing to do, however. When trying to determine whether potential team members have this capability, an indirect approach may be best. I believe a place to start is to look at your organization's remote workers or telecommuters, because their work characteristics are similar. Human resources professionals have spent a lot of time trying to figure out which employees they will allow to telecommute or work remotely. I argue that team members who can effectively telecommute also have the ability to effectively switch work modalities as necessary in the agile project environment. They are able to work with minimal guidance in an unstructured environment, they know how to use technology to their advantage, and they can deliver the results necessary to keep the project moving.

Technical Skills Versus Adaptability

When assembling a classic project team, the project manager or sponsor will generally rank technical skills as the number-one requirement for hiring a new team member. Soft skills, such as flexibility and adaptability, are not make-or-break hiring criteria, though they may act as a tiebreaker between two candidates with identical technical skills. This makes sense because once the primary planning process is complete, project execution becomes dominant, and that's when having the right technical resources counts. The key here, though, is that in the classic environment, the project plan (including resource requirements) is generally stable.

In the agile environment, the large amount of uncertainty produces frequent changes in the plan, so project teams must be flexible enough to deal with these direction changes in an efficient manner. This fact alone elevates the importance of "adaptability" on the hiring criteria spectrum (see Figure 6-1). To take this thought one step further into the agile realm, consider that a single change in the project plan could obviate the need for a particular type of expertise altogether. If you've just hired someone with that specific expertise, and only that expertise, then you've got a problem. What are you going to do with that person? Hopefully, the people you hire are adaptable in both attitude and skills. By attitude, I mean that they are willing to work in areas outside of their primary expertise for the benefit of the team (many people refuse to do this). And, of course, they should have actual skills in other areas that will benefit the team.

When selecting people for your agile team, you really want people who have broad technical skills and an attitude of adaptability. This

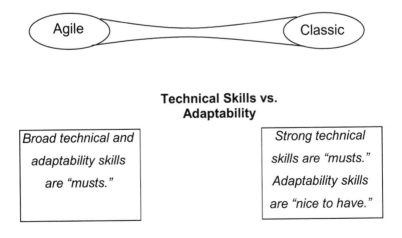

Figure 6-1. The hiring criteria in an agile versus classic project management.

combination of skills gives you the best chance of weaving them into the agile project team, as well as having them make meaningful and enthusiastic contributions.

This idea of adaptability may be so important in some agile projects that candidates with strong adaptability skills can arguably be elevated above those with superior technical skills. Those people who can develop and nourish the network of ideas and activities that make up the agile project are the core of your project team. They must, by definition, have broad skills and demonstrate adaptiveness for the simple reason that they are tasked with performing so many different functions. These functions include pulling together information from many sources, organizing it in the context of the project, and then turning it into the next steps that will move the project forward. Another way to look at it is that purely technical skills can be outsourced to any number of firms or free agents, but your core team cannot.

Agile Strategy

Outsource specific technical activities that are not necessarily hubs in the network of the project plan, and therefore are purely support for the rest of the project.

Developing a high-performing team is never easy, but it can be exhilarating if you are successful. The agile project environment presents its own unique challenges in the team-building area. Hopefully, you've gained some ideas that will help your team move to the next level.

Summary

❑ The ability to create networks is a valuable and uncommon skill for an agile team member.

❑ The agile team must be able to deal with changes in the project and must be able to drive changes in the organization.

❑ Find people for the agile team with the uncommon skill of being able to reinvent their organizations.

❑ Making the organizational changes dictated by the project team will ultimately lead to more agility in the overall organization.

❑ Agile team members will need to continually switch between working together and working alone.

❑ Adaptability may be more important than technical expertise on the agile team.

❑ Purely technical skills can always be outsourced.

7

PLANNING FOR AGILITY

Planning is usually one of the most painful, undervalued, and even vilified project management activities in the agile environment. Why? Project managers are most likely attempting to apply a classic planning process when they need an agile one. This chapter examines some of the key characteristics of planning required in an agile environment and how to recognize them, reduce the pain, and enhance the value of planning.

Today's projects are urgent, exciting, and critical to business success—and they provoke different spoken and unspoken feelings about planning: "We need to move fast out of the gate or we'll risk losing out to the competition," or "Spending up-front time planning will slow us down. I already know what to do, so let me go start doing it!"

On the flip side, you will rarely find an experienced professional who is 100 percent against any sort of planning activity. "We need a plan that will guide us to our destination. In fact, a good plan is almost indispensable," or "I wouldn't agree to even start work on a project without a plan." These reflect some of the supportive feelings about planning.

So where is the disconnect? On the one hand, planning is a waste of time. On the other, it's a must do. The answer lies in recognizing that business and projects have changed. Nowadays there's incredible urgency to move fast. There is also project uncertainty, which makes us nervous about solidifying requirements or committing to a schedule. Our common sense tells us that we obviously need a plan, but our experience tells us that there is not enough value added for the effort expended, and furthermore, the plan may come back to bite us. We need agility—and planning seems to be an obstacle to obtaining it.

Classic planning conjures up images of large meetings, work breakdown structures, Gantt charts, resource loading, all sorts of swags, and long-range commitments. This may be a slight exaggeration, and I don't want to belittle this type of planning because it is highly effective for managing projects in which the basic steps are well known. Installing and validating a new piece of production test equipment is a good example. We know how to manage this process, but since this is a new piece of equipment, it will be slightly different from the last installation project. In this classic environment, there is no good reason why we shouldn't be able to create and commit to a detailed plan of this type.

But what about the agile environment, where we are trying to create something totally new and nothing similar has been done before? Does the classic planning process still make sense? Probably not. We shouldn't be spending a lot of up-front effort planning six or more months out when a discovery or decision made in the next three weeks could change everything. This is an important point, but often it's hard to recognize, especially when the level of uncertainty is not clear.

Agile Strategy

Only extend your detailed planning into the foreseeable future, to the next milestone or decision point, but not much further. Extended plans are risky and can frustrate team members being asked to create them.

To the project manager, a new project may seem similar to previous efforts, but to the technical team it may present totally new challenges. Since the project manager is not usually the technical expert, the *level* of project uncertainty should be discussed and agreed to early in the planning process by all key players. By making this effort up-front, the project manager is helping to set the tone regarding the planning methodology for the remainder of the project—specifically, how frequently or infrequently planning activities will take place. Essentially, the team should be expected to have detailed plans, but only up to the point where the project direction is still clearly visible. Once we reach the point where project uncertainty starts to blur the course, we will limit planning to high-level pathways. For example, let's say that we plan to produce a small lot of prototype circuit boards in three months. The next stage of the project is testing, which will ideally be at the final product level but may have to be at the subassembly level, and each of these pathways have specific and unique details that need to be planned out. The decision on which path to take depends on the delivery of a series of other components by outside suppliers who are running into difficulties and can't currently commit to a delivery date. Classic PM methods would teach us that we should have a detailed task list for completion of the circuit boards, as well as for each contingent pathway (final or subassembly-level testing). In the agile case, we also have a detailed timeline for completion of the circuit boards, but we only want a high-level understanding of the requirements for doing either final product or subassembly testing at this time, not the detailed task planning. In this way, the team will not get frustrated trying to create details around something that is too far out in the future, while the project manager will still be getting solid plans for the near term. Once the uncertainty around the outside supplier clears, the team would know which path to take and create the necessary detailed plans.

Agile Strategy

Set the tone for the project planning process by facilitating a team discussion on the *level* of technical and business uncertainty associated with the project. This, in turn, will help team members understand the scope and frequency of planning efforts throughout the project (i.e., high uncertainty leads to small but frequent detailed planning efforts, while low uncertainty leads to larger and less frequent detailed planning activities).

This does not mean that we can ditch the planning effort for projects that involve uncertainty, only that we have to plan for agility in different ways. Let's look at a few dimensions of the planning process and how they differ in classic and agile environments.

Activities Versus Achievements

Classical planning is based on activities. Once the key activities are identified, then resources are assigned, effort and duration are estimated, and a sequence is created. The problem with this approach for an agile project is that it is based on the team's ability to accurately identify all of the activities in the project. For projects that have been done many times before, it is relatively easy to identify the major activities, and in fact, these projects often start out their planning effort with a template from the previous project. For projects on the technology development end of the spectrum, it's quite a different story.

Agile Strategy

When planning an agile project, ask team members to identify the achievements or milestones required to complete the project, rather than the detailed tasks.

Projects that operate on the edge of new technology tend to take a zigzag course toward their destination (see Figure 7-1). The technical leaders know the general direction they must go and the sequence of milestones that must be achieved. What they don't usually know is the exact path or pathways that they will take. For these reasons, it is somewhat impractical to attempt to construct a timeline based on *activities*. An attempt to do so may backfire by frustrating everyone in-

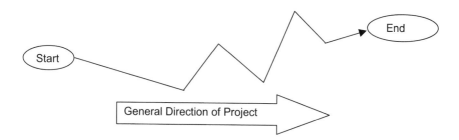

Figure 7-1. Projects that operate on the edge of technology tend to take a zigzag course toward their objectives.

volved. A more practical approach is to construct your timeline based on *achievements,* since those are the things that the technical team will be focused on (see Figure 7-2). This is a subtle but critical difference between planning using agile methods versus classical methods.

The upside of activity-based planning is that you are able to mechanically capture, fairly accurately, both the sequence and duration dimensions of your timeline. While achievement-based planning only captures the sequence dimension, in the agile environment, achievements (or milestones) are made up of several yet-to-be-defined activities, and because there are multiple possible pathways leading to each achievement, there is no mechanical method to construct a good bottom-up time estimate. This leaves us with the top-down method for estimating duration, which works rather well for an experienced team. I've found that technical people, while often resistant to formal project management, are actually very good at estimating durations of

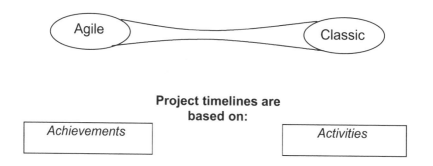

Figure 7-2. The basis of timelines in an agile versus classic environment.

achievements. They don't like the restrictions associated with committing to a specific sequence of activities since they know that sequence will change. However, they will commit to achieving a milestone in a certain amount of time if you don't bother them too much with how they are going to do it (see Figure 7-3).

Agile Strategy

Use the top-down method for resource and duration estimation rather than the traditional bottom-up method.

Estimates Versus Commitments

The key to this type of estimating is to ask for a *commitment* rather than just a top-down *estimate*. Asking for a commitment brings the business dimension into clearer focus for the team member by emphasizing the impact of not meeting your commitment. It also forces people to think through their approach more carefully, perhaps breaking it down into smaller achievements, which are, in turn, easier to get a handle on. Technical and creative environments are tricky quarters to plan within. The individuals who excel in these areas need room to explore and experiment with various ideas. The very concept of a project plan is at odds with the creative environment. Approaching the planning effort by asking for top-down commitments for reaching the next achievement/milestone creates a win–win situation. You, the

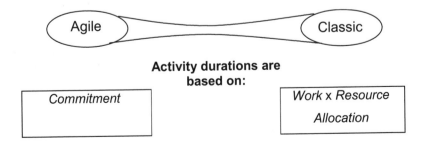

Figure 7-3. The basis of activity durations in an agile versus classic environment.

project manager, get the information that you need to manage the project, and the technical expert will see a planning process that doesn't restrict his creative side—and may actually help him to add valuable structure to the technical approach. Finally, gaining commitments from individual team members is a great way to pull the whole team together and ensure that they are all rowing in the same direction.

Agile Strategy

Combine your request to individuals for a top-down duration estimate on a milestone with a request for a commitment to meet that estimate.

The process of building an achievement-based schedule using committed durations is not necessarily easy, but it will be more effective in an agile environment. Commitments tend to be dependent on each other, so the whole team needs to work together and become engaged for this process to work. Rather than spending energy to estimate resource allocations and durations along a single sequence of activities, as is done in the classic planning method, the team will find itself developing a primary pathway and several alternative pathways. They will be identifying decision points that will drive or eliminate certain pathways. And they will begin strategizing their overall approach to the project. For these reasons, a network diagram is often a better mechanism than the more common Gantt chart for depicting the high-level view of the agile project.

Agile Strategy

Use network diagrams rather than Gantt charts to show the multiple pathways and corresponding decision points in the agile project.

Network Diagrams

Network diagrams (see Figure 7-4) work well for agile projects because they can convey the overall project landscape without much

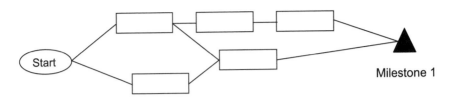

Milestone 1

Figure 7-4. Network diagrams provide a high-level view of a project, especially when there are multiple pathways and decision points, without going into great detail.

detail, which is what we need at the outset of an agile project. Focusing on the details is effective for a relatively predictable project, but is often a waste of time when operating in an environment of constant change. If a project reaches a decision point and goes one way instead of another, then the effort to define and estimate details along the unused pathway is wasted. Because we know that much of our plan (prepared as a network diagram) will not be used, details in the agile project are worked out only as the certainty of taking a specific pathway is solidified, thereby minimizing wasted planning effort.

Combining Network Diagrams and Gantt Charts

In the classic project, the up-front planning effort focuses on identifying project details along the primary path, and so the project manager's main duty after completion of the plan is managing the project execution. That's not necessarily the case in an agile environment. The agile project still needs to do detailed planning to be successful; it's just not all done in the initial planning effort. Up-front agile planning revolves around identifying pathways and decision points, but the details evolve as the project progresses and uncertainty diminishes. While the network diagram lays out the high-level plan, the Gantt chart can be put into play to document the details of a specific pathway (see Figure 7-5).

In the agile project, the advance planning effort can be reduced to a high-level end-to-end plan (network diagram), plus a detailed plan (Gantt chart) looking out to the foreseeable horizon. The detailed part should consider two dimensions. The first is related to the uncertainty

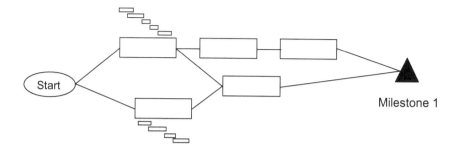

Figure 7-5. Gantt chart overlaid on a network diagram.

at hand. For example, only provide detailed plans leading up to a critical decision point so the team doesn't waste energy planning to go down one road only to later find out that it's a dead end. The second dimension is related to time. For example, you may decide to always have a detailed plan looking three months out no matter what, so that other team members, support organizations, and management can make their plans accordingly.

Agile Strategy

Create your project plan in two parts: a high-level, end-to-end network diagram, plus a commitment-based Gantt chart leading to foreseeable milestones.

This leads us to a critical concept regarding planning for agile projects. You need to make planning a normal part of managing the project. Plans must be constantly updated based on the latest information that becomes available throughout the project's duration. Another way to think of planning for agile project management is that it is a constant but low-effort activity, rather than the traditional high-effort up-front activity (see Figure 7-6).

As further illustrated in Figure 7-7, the overall effort allocated to project planning (the area under the curve) may be very similar to the classic methods that you are probably more familiar with. It's just that your efforts are allocated differently over the course of the project.

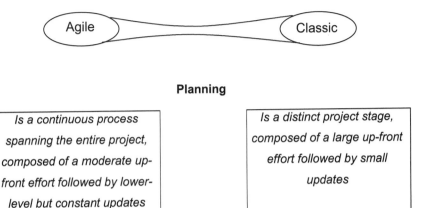

Planning

Is a continuous process spanning the entire project, composed of a moderate up-front effort followed by lower-level but constant updates	*Is a distinct project stage, composed of a large up-front effort followed by small updates*

Figure 7-6. The approach to planning in an agile versus classic environment.

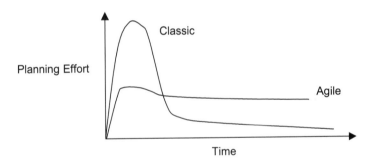

Figure 7-7. Planning effort over time using agile and classic planning methods.

Agile Strategy

Plan to make planning a continuing effort throughout your project, rather than a single, large effort up-front.

The project manager leads the planning activity, and his key challenge in this area is to show the project team the value of planning in an agile environment. Your team needs to understand what to expect if you want their buy-in and support for the process. Management also needs to understand this new paradigm so that they can make decisions in the proper context. An up-front discussion with the entire team on how the planning process will be tuned for agility is critical.

An Agile Planning Tool

There is one planning tool that I've found to be exceptionally effective when used on the agile project. This is the Project Data Sheet (PDS). The PDS is a one- to three-page executive summary of a project that covers both classic and agile elements of project management required for success, such as a project description, objectives, milestones, timeline, and resource estimates. It gets the job done and is "light" enough that it doesn't inflict undo pain on the team, which is exactly what we want in an agile environment.

First and foremost, the Project Data Sheet is a communication tool. By summarizing all of the critical characteristics of your project into the concise PDS format, you can easily share your project ideas with management, contributors, other project managers, and program managers to gain their support and feedback. If you find yourself running projects in an agile environment, it is likely that you have numerous smaller projects taking place simultaneously. Some projects are independent but many are interdependent. To keep the many projects aligned with business objectives and make the most efficient use of valuable resources, it is important that all project managers be able to concisely describe their project. Creating a "deck of PDS's" allows management to readily assess the overall project portfolio without having to go into a question-and-answer session with each project manager just to get basic information. Everyone is stretched for time. Using the PDS format will greatly reduce the time and energy required of the project stakeholders.

Agile Strategy

Use the Project Data Sheet format to create an executive summary of the project. The PDS, in turn, will provide a valuable communication tool in keeping the project on task to meet technical and business objectives.

The second major benefit of using the PDS format is that it is short and concise, unlike the comprehensive planning templates commonly created during classic PM (see Figure 7-8). When backed up by a detailed Gantt chart through the next major milestones, the PDS makes it significantly easier for the project manager to maintain the high-level and detailed parts of the plan as the agile project progresses. How many times have you seen teams put together fantastic in-depth plans that essentially become out-of-date as soon as the first unplanned event happens?

An example of the Project Data Sheet is included at the end of this chapter. You can customize the template provided to encompass other key project elements that are unique to your environment. The main point to remember is that you're trying to create an executive summary that can be quickly scanned for critical information.

There's no doubt that project planning is a time-consuming yet valuable task. The unpredictability of the agile environment and very nature of innovative projects makes planning even more challenging. However, before any value of project planning can even be demonstrated, your project team must buy into and support the process. This chapter has looked at some alternatives to the standard project plan-

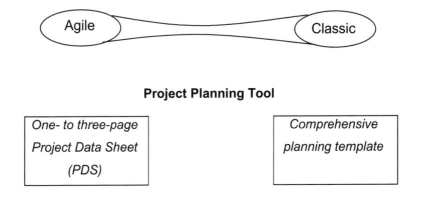

Figure 7-8. The basic planning tools in an agile versus classic environment.

ning process that will help you to get that support from your technical team and, subsequently, add real value to project planning on the fuzzy front end.

Summary

❑ By discussing the level of project uncertainty early in the planning process, you'll set the tone for planning the rest of the project.

❑ Agile planning is based on achievements and commitments to meeting them.

❑ Network diagrams can clearly show the multiple pathways and decision points in an agile project.

❑ The up-front planning effort should consist of a high-level network diagram showing pathways and decision points, plus a detailed Gantt chart looking out to the foreseeable horizon.

❑ Make low-level planning a regular part of the project management culture.

❑ Concise Project Data Sheets are an effective and "light" planning tool for agile projects.

Project Data Sheet Workflow

This section describes how to use the Project Data Sheet (PDS) when initiating a new project. This process will guide you through the fundamentals of project planning in a logical and concise manner, subsequently creating an executive summary of your project.

The PDS is a communication tool. By summarizing the critical characteristics of your project into the PDS format, you can easily and expeditiously share your project plans with stakeholders (e.g., sponsor, functional management, team members, other project managers) to obtain their support and/or feedback.

The PDS is designed so that individual sections can be easily included or omitted from the final output. Also, there are many different types of projects, and one process does not fit them all. You are encouraged to customize this process where applicable by modifying or adding sections.

Creating the PDS is an iterative process. It generally works well when a small core group (sometimes only the project manager) creates the first draft and then reviews/discusses it with the larger team, perhaps at a project kickoff meeting or project start-up workshop.

An electronic copy of this workflow and template can be downloaded from www.xocp.com.

Identify the Project and Project Team

Uniquely identifying the project itself, as well as the project team, is a simple step toward eliminating confusion and setting project accountability. In the PDS, only the names of the respective individuals are included. It is also a good idea to clarify the roles and responsibilities of these individuals; however, this should be done in a separate document from the PDS, such as the Communications Plan, so that adequate detail can be included.

Project Manager	This is the person responsible for managing the overall project.
Project Sponsor	This is the primary person who wants the project done and who is authorizing that resources be expended to complete it.
Team Members	These are the people who are contributing to the project.

Define the Project

A well-defined project sets clear expectations for the project manager, project team, project sponsors, and functional management. Everyone needs to know why they are doing the project and what they hope to accomplish. A good project definition can also head off confusion down the road by identifying, up-front, any ambiguous areas and challenges. It clearly differentiates what "is" and "is not" included in the project.

Why are we doing this project?	This is the project Problem Statement. It frames the project context for people not intimately involved. Since not all projects are undertaken to address a particular problem, this section may be omitted if appropriate or combined with the next section. However, if there is a particular problem that this project is intended to solve, then a problem statement is very valuable. The problem statement should be included in the *project description* section of the Project Data Sheet.
What is this project trying to accomplish?	Write one or more high-level Objective statements describing what you hope to accomplish by undertaking this project. These statements are succinct and are essentially describing the scope of the project. To aid in bounding the scope, you may want to include an "Is/Is not" list to help minimize future scope creep. These statements should be copied to the *project objectives* section of the Project Data Sheet.
How will the team approach the project?	This section should capture the technical and/or business approach to the project at a high-level. Discuss the methodologies that will be used to complete the project (not the ones used to manage the project), as well as how and where work will get done. These statements should be copied to the *approach* section of the Project Data Sheet.
How will you know when you're done?	This isn't always clear, especially in a technology or product development environment. However, defining your success criteria will aid in planning the overall project. You should start with the above-mentioned Objective statement(s) and translate them into major Deliverables that, when complete, will indicate that a key milestone has been reached or the project itself is complete. For projects that may be open-ended, these major deliverables should reflect your thought process in approaching the project. While milestones may change as the project progresses, it is still important to capture the general direction that the project is taking so that resources can be planned, dependencies identified, etc. The information collected should be copied to the *deliverables* section of the Project Data Sheet.
What are your external dependencies?	Identify the events external to your project that must happen before a part or all of the project can be completed. Pay special attention to those dependencies that could prevent you from completing any of the steps in this Project Data Sheet workflow. If there's an external dependency,

such as the marketing strategy, that must be completed before you can properly define your project, then that should raise a red flag and tell you that your project is not being set up for success.

Determine a target date by which you need the dependency resolved in order to make your project plan work.

All dependencies should be discussed with the appropriate owners of the events that you are dependent on so that they know your time requirements and they are aware that they are a potential bottleneck to your project.

The information you collect should be copied to the *dependencies* section of the Project Data Sheet.

| Classify your boundary constraints | There are three core dimensions of any project—scope, schedule, and resources—and each has boundaries that either can or cannot be constrained as the project progresses. Ideally, the project would be completed exactly according to the original plan, in which case there would be no need for this section at all. However, this usually isn't the case. You should assess your level of acceptable constraint during the definition and planning phases for two reasons. It will help identify up-front problems with the project plan, and it will facilitate decision making done "in the heat of the moment" during the project execution phase.

For each core project dimension, select one of the following levels of constraint that is acceptable and agreed to by the project sponsor and project manager:

Fixed: No significant change from the original project definition and plan. Be as specific as possible in identifying sub-elements within a core dimension because it's very difficult and often not realistic to fix every minute detail.

Limited: Can be changed from the original plan within limits. If this level is selected, then you should also be as specific as possible in identifying the sub-elements in question, as well as specifying the limit.

Flexible: Can be changed as needed.

If more than one dimension is identified as "fixed," it should raise a red flag. This could indicate a lack of maneuvering room for the team while executing the project. Projects operating in an agile environment should not have any fixed dimensions.

Constraint levels and limits should be reflected in the *boundary constraints* section of the Project Data Sheet. |
| Describe your project | Now that you have thought through all of the above-listed elements of the project, you should have the necessary |

information to start a short project description. The Project Description should be one or two paragraphs, and it should be able to stand on its own. This is your project "elevator pitch." As the project manager, you should be able to comfortably and concisely describe your project to anyone, either verbally or in writing. If you cannot write a short project description at this time, then you should be cautious about moving forward with the project—there are still holes in your project definition. Having an incomplete project definition isn't a showstopper. Often project teams need to do some investigatory work before they can fully define their project. This is okay, but you should remember to return here to complete the project description.

At this time, your project description should tell the reader *why* you are doing the project and *what* you hope to accomplish. (Note: The project description is not complete at this time. You will add to the project description later in this workflow.)

Plan the Project

Now that you have defined your project, the next step is to plan your project. In the ideal world, this is a serial process—planning comes after definition. However, in reality, time pressures often force these steps to happen in parallel. In fact, some project managers prefer to do them in parallel because it helps the overall thought process. This is fine. The mistake that you do not want to make is to totally skip the project definition step and just start out by planning the project. This would be like starting to design a new product without any specifications. There is a high chance that what you create will not be what the customer wants!

Network diagram

If your approach to the project involves decision points, iterations, or multiple pathways, then it will be beneficial to have a separate network diagram since these characteristics are difficult to depict and read in a Gantt chart. A milestone-level network diagram is an excellent tool for illustrating the general approach to a project.

Identify the project milestones
    A milestone is a point of noteworthy accomplishment in your project. These are the points that will appear on your high-level project plans and progress reports to management. A milestone is not the same as a task in that its duration is equal to zero. Milestones are those points in time immediately following the completion of a task.

The first step is to identify your milestones. Start this process with the project *deliverables* (defined previously) since the completion of a deliverable is considered a milestone.

Examples of other milestones might be:

- ❑ When you exit an iterative loop in your plan, such as when a product finally passes a suite of tests
- ❑ The completion point of the whole project, as well as any subprojects
- ❑ Other major project accomplishments

Identify the project decision points	Decision points are those places in your project plan where you need to decide which of multiple possible pathways to take. These are not the day-to-day decisions that are made in the course of performing a task, but rather the decisions that will dictate which task to pursue next. Examples of decision points might be: ❑ The pass/fail point of a test that indicates whether to proceed or to loop back and modify the product before testing again ❑ The fork between two or more pathways, where you need to decide which one(s) to pursue
Lay out the milestones and decision points	Lay out your milestones and decision points in a sequential fashion. (Note: A decision point is also a milestone.)
Connect the milestones and decision points	Use arrows to connect the milestones and decision points, as well as to show the direction of the sequence.
Assign ownership to milestones	Work with the project team to assign ownership to the various milestones. While any single person may not own all of the detailed tasks leading up a milestone, it is still beneficial to assign ownership to milestones. Identify milestone ownership on the network diagram.
Assign target dates	Assign target dates to milestones and decision points, if known. For example, if you have *fixed* or *limited* your schedule (when you classified your boundary constraints), then this would be a guideline for assigning target dates. For milestones within loops or decision points at the end of a loop, identify the target date for the first pass. It is not critical to assign dates to all milestones at this point. The primary goal of the network diagram is to depict the approach to the project. The next section, timeline, will focus specifically on assigning dates to all milestones, after which you may return to this section and fill in the missing dates.

| Assign target iterations through loops | Estimate the number of times you expect to go through a loop before exiting it. Iteration through a loop is something that teams get a good grasp on only through experience, but it has a potentially enormous impact on the timeline and is an excellent discussion point. As such, it is important to include here. |

Timeline

The timeline is your best tool for communicating the project duration in total, as well as between milestones. For the purposes of the Project Data Sheet, which is intended to be an executive summary of the project, it is only necessary to use milestones (not detailed tasks) in depicting the timeline. A task-level Gantt chart is often very valuable, but it should be created as a separate document, either attached to the PDS or included as a separate section in an overall project plan.

Lay out the milestones, decision points, and external dependencies	Lay out your milestones, decision points, and dependencies in a sequential fashion on a timeline of appropriate scale. (Note: A decision point is also a milestone.)
Assign fixed dates	Review your project constraints for any specific dates that were assigned to milestones as fixed. The most likely fixed milestone is the project completion milestone, though interim milestones may also be specifically fixed as needed. For instance, if a specific individual must start another project on a specific date, then any milestone that he is responsible for must be completed prior to that date. Identify the dates of fixed milestones on your timeline.
Assigned limited dates	Review your project constraints for any specific dates that were assigned to milestones as limited. Identify the limited dates on your timeline with your early target date and show their limit.
Insert dates for external dependencies	Review your project's external dependencies for any timeline-related dependencies. For example, let's say a piece of test equipment is being transferred from another facility and it needs to be online before a specific milestone can be reached. This would be an external dependency if the transfer was not being managed as part of the project. It would not be a dependency if it was part of the project, since you would be expected to plan for it. Identify the target dates for external dependencies on the timeline.

Assign owner-ship to mile-stones	If you have previously created a network diagram, then you will have already done this step. If not, then work with the project team now to assign ownership to the various milestones. While any single person may not own all of the detailed tasks leading up a milestone, it is still beneficial to assign ownership to milestones.
	Identify milestone ownership on the timeline.
Assign dates to remaining milestones	Work with the owners of the various milestones to assign target completion dates to each. For the purposes of the Project Data Sheet, it is appropriate to use a top-down estimate since the timeline only consists of milestones at this time. However, this information can be updated later if a more detailed bottom-up Gantt chart and duration estimate is created.
	Identify the dates of the remaining milestones on the timeline.

Resources

This section will consist of a top-down rolling estimate of resources required for the project, including people and money.

List the team	List the team members in the Resource column.
Determine your time horizon	Determine how large of a rolling window you want to capture resource estimates for. It usually works best when done quarterly (e.g., 3, 6, 9, or 12 months). Don't try to estimate further out than you can reasonably foresee, because it could create frustration among the team and give false impressions of the actual resources required.
	Delete any extra columns so that you do not leave blank columns.
Make a top-down FTE estimate	Work with each individual team member to create a top-down resource estimate, based on the timeline above, in FTE-months, for each month in your rolling window. An FTE (full time equivalent) is equal to one person working full-time. An FTE month is equal to one person working full-time for one month. Depending on how you track costs, contractors and consultants may be included here or in the money resources section below.
	Enter the FTE estimates for each team member into the table.
Make a top-down money estimate	Work with the entire team to estimate the amount of money (outside of salaries for the team) that will be required to support the project. New equipment purchases, prototypes, and travel would be included here.

	Enter the total project money expenditures into the table.
Total the resources	Add up the monthly resource estimates and total (rolling window) resource estimates.

Risks

Identify project risks	Identify potential risks to the project's success. A detailed risk management plan should be a separate document or section in an overall project plan. (See Chapter 8 on Risk Management for details on risk identification.) For the purposes of the Project Data Sheet, the risks only need to be listed. List the top risks in the *risk* section of the Project Data Sheet.

Description completion

Update your project description	You now have two more elements with which to update your Project Description—time and resource estimates. Rewrite your Project Description to tell the reader *why* you are doing the project, *what* you hope to accomplish, *when* you expect the project to be completed, and *how much* it will cost. You may also make reference to the dependencies, constraints, and risks, which are described in more detail in other sections of the PDS.

Change history

Record change history of the Project Data Sheet	As one of the primary communication tools for the project, the Project Data Sheet should be maintained as the various project characteristics change during project execution. When modifying the PDS, it is good practice to save previous versions, either electronically or hard copy, so that you have a solid trail of changes that can be reviewed if necessary. Also, this history can be valuable when reviewing the lessons learned after a project has been completed. Record the date and a brief description whenever the PDS is changed.

Template for the Product Data Sheet (PDS)

Project Name   Project Data Sheet

Project manager: *name of person*
Project sponsor: *name of person*
Project team: *names of team member 1, team member 2, team member 3, . . .*

Description:

Your project description should tell the reader *why* you are doing the project (problem statement), *what* you hope to accomplish, *when* you expect the project to be completed, and *how much* it will cost. *(Note: Complete this section last.)*

Objectives:

Write one or more high-level Objective statements describing what you hope to accomplish by undertaking this project. These statements are succinct and are essentially describing the scope of the project. To aid in bounding the scope, you may want to include an "Is/Is not" list to help minimize future scope creep.

Approach:

Describe your technical and/or business approach to the project.

Deliverables:

Write one or more deliverables (nouns) that, when complete, will indicate that a major milestone has been reached or that the project itself has been completed.

Dependencies:

Describe external activities/projects that must be completed before you can complete this project (or a part of this project).

Boundary constraints:

Identify the level of constraint that the project team and sponsor agree to, for each major project dimension.

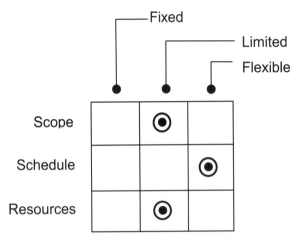

Risks:

List the top project risks. See Chapter 8 on Risk Management for details on risk identification.

Network diagram:

Insert a graphic showing the sequence of milestones, decision points, loops, and target competition dates. Also indicate (using initials) the person responsible for each milestone.

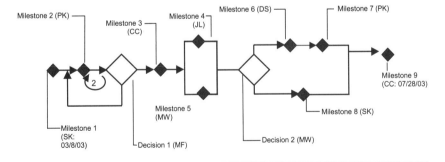

Timeline/Milestones:

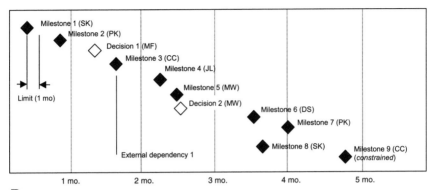

Resources:

Provide an estimate of the resources (people and money) required to complete this project, as described above. People should be estimated using FTE (full time equivalent) months.

Resource:	S	O	N	D	J	F	M	A	M	J	J	A	Total
Project manager													
Team member #1													
Team member #2													
Team member #3													
Total FTE months													
Money ($)													

Change History

Date:	Description of change:
Today's date	As issued

8

APPROACHING RISK IN AN AGILE ENVIRONMENT

Risk management is one of those areas where the rubber meets the road. Do it well, and you will avoid the numerous potholes and roadblocks that inevitably pop up in most projects. Do it poorly, and you will find yourself in crisis-management mode more often than project-execution mode. This chapter looks at the subtle differences in the mechanics of risk planning in an agile environment versus a classic one. It also covers the not-so-subtle attitudes of how risk management is often perceived in one environment versus the other.

Let's start off by taking a look at a hypothetical business scenario and reviewing the potential impact of classic and agile risk management approaches.

Time to Market

Getting to market as fast as possible is, perhaps, the most frequently cited project management urgency. And this is for a good reason. Financial analysts everywhere are influenced by the "first mover" advantage. Simply put, the first-mover advantage states that the first company to market with a new product or feature will grab the majority of the market share. Of course, there are many other variables that can affect the market share captured by a new product, but the absence of a competitive product is very compelling.

Imagine the business advantages of beating your competition to market and enjoying a temporary monopoly (of sorts) until they catch up. You lock in your current customers, and then convert some of your competitor's customers, thereby increasing your market share. Your increased volume gives you economies of scale and better terms with your suppliers, thus, driving down your costs. You have pricing flexibility, which leads to higher margins. Your project breakeven time is drastically reduced, making future projects that much easier to justify. And the lifetime return on the project has just shot up dramatically, increasing your company's bottom line. All in all, being first to market allows you to create a whirlwind of enthusiasm around your product and within your company.

Product lifecycles are continuing to shorten, and getting to market within the target window (of opportunity) often determines the overall success of both the project and product. By classic PM standards, the *project* can be successful (if the scope is delivered on schedule and within cost), while the *product* is actually a failure. Running too many of these so-called "successful" projects will eventually bring down the whole organization. When presented with a business scenario that requires a course change for the project, you need to remember to equate the project to the current business realities rather than the previously determined, and possibly out-of-date, project boundaries. Now let's see what the picture might look like if you are beaten to market and your competition steals even a small percentage of your customers.

First, assuming your products are essentially equivalent, you have little chance of gaining back any lost market share until your next product release. Your customers needed a product. You couldn't supply it when they needed it (or perceived a need for it), so they went to your competitor (with a little nudging from their sales/marketing efforts), end of story. Second, your reduced volume puts you at a disadvantage with your suppliers, potentially reducing your margins and making it harder to hit the financials for the product. Third, your project breakeven just moved out to the right, making the justification for the next product release that much harder for management to swallow. Ironically, when you are beaten to market, you need to be especially agile in bouncing back to win the next race and can't afford to be spending excess time justifying follow-on projects. Fourth, the lifetime return on your project may have just gone negative. And, guess what, you probably can't just cancel the product because you are committed to the customers that you have managed to retain. You are going to be producing a money-losing product until you can replace it with a better one. Hopefully, you'll win that race.

A more and more common tactic for accelerating timelines is to reduce the scope (i.e., features) of a project/release with the promise of quickly adding the dropped features in the next release (see Figure 8-1). Typically, a move like this is in reaction to one of two broad situations: First, something has happened in the marketplace (external to the project). It could be that a marketing manager catches word of an impending competitive move. He then comes to the project manager asking what can be done to finish up and get to market as soon as possible. Or second, it could be something internal to the project itself, such as technical obstacles that are creating significant troubles

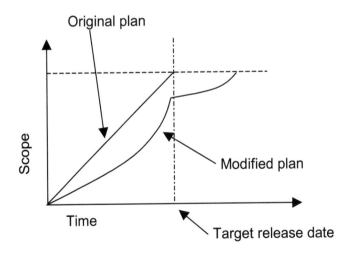

Figure 8-1. Reducing scope to get to market earlier usually extends the overall time and cost needed to get to the original scope.

in one part of the project and not others. As a result, the project manager has incentive to move forward and complete the project (minus the one trouble area). This is a good example of integrating the *project* and the *business,* because to decide on a course of action, the team must consider all of the project dimensions, plus the market analysis, manufacturing cost, scheduling viability, technical support availability for the initial release and upgrade, the overall financial picture, and any other relevant business elements. Usually, this route involves increasing the overall cost and timeline of the project to get to the same scope (as in your original plan), but these actions may be justified, depending on the outcome of the aforementioned analysis.

So, while a decision based solely on the project characteristics may point us in one direction, when the business dimensions are put into the mix, we are pointed in quite a different direction. Being able to make the right decisions in situations such as these is greatly enhanced if anticipated and planned for as part of a risk management strategy, rather than managed "on the fly" in a reactionary fashion. The classic risk management strategies of mitigation and contingency are applicable in the agile environment, but with slight modifications.

Mitigation

Mitigation plans can be thought of as doing extra work, beyond the original plan, in an effort to prevent the risk event from ever happening. Note that this is not usually chosen as an approach to address a competitive (i.e., external) risk, but it is commonly used for technical (i.e., internal) ones, such as in our example of a technical difficulty in part of the project. This is an effective way to address a risk, assuming that the added costs can be justified. Certainly, if the costs of mitigating a risk outweigh the benefits, then it does not make sense to implement a mitigation strategy.

The key to effectively using mitigation plans in an agile environment is early identification of the risk. The reason is simply due to the time horizon under which such a plan can be created and implemented. In the classic paradigm, we may develop a detailed Gantt

chart up-front for a six-month project, thus leaving a pretty long period in which to identify risks and develop mitigation plans. In the
agile scenario for the same-length project, we may have a network
diagram with six major milestones, but only a detailed Gantt chart
through the next milestone. If the risk is within the window of the
next milestone, there may not be adequate time to efficiently create
and implement a mitigation plan. However, if the identified risk is
three milestones out on the network diagram, there will be quite a bit
of time to develop a mitigation strategy that can be woven into the
detailed plans leading up to that milestone.

Agile Strategy

When using mitigation plans in conjunction with the agile planning
approach, be cognizant of the time horizon available in which to plan
and implement the mitigation, once the risk is identified.

Contingency

Contingency plans can be thought of as subsets of an overall project
plan that get filed away. They are only used if the specific risk event
does occur. The objective of a contingency plan is to neutralize the
impact of a risk to your project, and it can be just as important as the
primary project plan for high-priority risks.

The key to contingency planning is to be able to identify those
few risks that are worth planning for. After all, it is not efficient to
create contingency plans around every identified risk. The ability to
categorize the identified risks as a "high enough" priority is necessary
to make this process work.

The general goal of contingency plans is to develop alternate pathways to circumvent potential problems, if they should present themselves. This lends itself well to the agile planning approach of using
network diagrams to map the various possible pathways since analysis
of these pathways can help you plan for the potential direction that
the project will take. In fact, you could say that contingency plans are

integrated into the overall agile plan right from the start, albeit at a high level, where the contingency is equivalent to an alternate path that the project may take at a predetermined decision point.

By standing back and studying all the possible project pathways, you are able to gain the 20,000-foot view necessary to take in the whole project. If you then assign weighting to each branch of a decision point, based on what is most likely to happen, not what you want to happen, you will start to see the higher-probability pathways emerge (see Figure 8-2). From here, you can take the necessary actions to guide the project forward. For example, a project manager may decide to extend the detailed planning process past the next foreseeable milestone or decision point, if there is a high enough probability that a particular pathway will be taken.

Agile Strategy

Prioritize the already-defined pathways of the network diagram so that you can focus your team's energy on the most likely paths.

Classic project planning is centered on creating a single, primary plan. When using this approach, contingency plans are generally focused on circumventing an obstacle, then getting back onto the primary plan. Since agile project planning involves looking at multiple possible project pathways, contingency planning involves more analy-

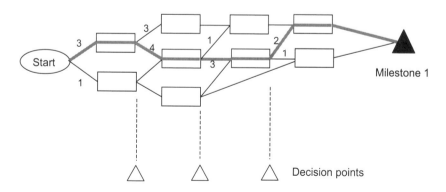

Figure 8-2. Network diagram with probability weighting assigned to various pathways.

sis of the pathways, so you can best guide the project toward the next milestone. It isn't necessarily focused on returning to the primary pathway. (See Figure 8-3.)

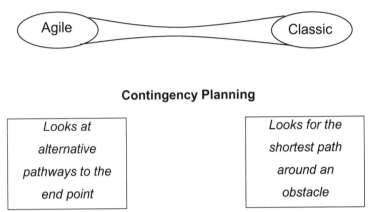

Figure 8-3. Contingency planning in an agile versus classic environment.

In the end, the classic and agile approaches to risk management are very similar. The core classic methods are very effective, and they need not be abandoned in the agile environment. However, the shorter, detailed planning horizon makes classic risk management methods more time-sensitive to implement when using the agile planning methodology. Agile projects are inherently more reactive due to the high uncertainty, and this is also true of agile risk management. This deficiency is strictly related to the shorter, detailed planning horizon, but it can be compensated for by some high-level anticipation of possible project pathways. The workflow at the end of this chapter provides a guideline for sequentially thinking through the mechanics of the risk management process. However, while having good mechanics around risk management is necessary for success, a potentially more critical element is the organization's attitude toward it.

Organizational Attitude Toward Changing the Plan

Perhaps the primary difference between classic and agile PM is in the organization's attitude toward changing the primary project plan via contingency plans. Classic PM expects the primary (i.e., initial) project plan to be pretty good. Functional areas plan their resources and other activities around the primary project plan and hardly give notice to the contingency plans, if they even exist. Thus, changes to the initial plan are not usually welcome news to management. Logically, management accepts the changes, but there is often the undercurrent of judgment that the project manager did not do his job well enough up-front, and that *that* is the real cause of the change.

An environment that implicitly views changes in the primary project plan as negative creates inherent delays in dealing with the issues that prompted the changes.

In the agile environment, we don't expect to stay with the original plan for the course of the project. We expect that the primary plan will point us in the right direction, but that course changes will be required to navigate the uncertain landscape (see Figure 8-4). Thus, when the project manager executes a contingency plan (i.e., diverts from the primary pathway), management is not surprised. There is more support, there is less questioning, and there is minimal delay in approving these key decisions.

In most companies, major project changes are a blood pressure–raising exercise that is frowned upon. Since there is a negative con-

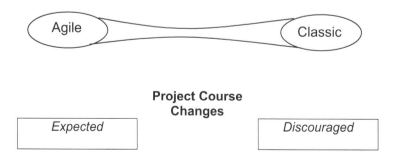

Agile   Classic

**Project Course
Changes**

Expected   Discouraged

Figure 8-4. Project course changes in an agile versus classic environment.

notation associated with these course changes, project managers, sponsors, and technical leaders alike are reluctant to champion them until it's too late. When these course changes do get under way, they're usually frantic and frustrating for the project team, creating more incentive to sweep the next one under the proverbial rug. It is for all of these reasons that course changes on projects are usually not as effective as they could be. To be successful, we need to break away from the stigma that change is bad, or is the result of bad planning. Creating, communicating, and discussing appropriate risk management plans is an effective way to do this. Creating them demonstrates a forward-looking project management perspective. Communicating them tends to pull in the interested stakeholders. And discussing them generates the energy and support necessary to make the plans happen.

Agile Strategy

Keep your team looking forward by working with them to develop network diagram–based contingency plans, and then communicate and discuss these with both your team and external stakeholders.

Agile PM calls for any number of possible business scenarios to be put in front of the project manager. As discussed previously in Chapter 3, you need to make the project the business. Visualize the benefits of getting to market first and the downfalls of coming in second. Let the project manager combine her intimate knowledge of the project with the business realities, and let her imagine how she will lead the team and company to success, including how she will manage risk. Encourage the use of appropriate mitigation and contingency planning. Get management sign-off on the risk pathways, and let the project manager run with them. Finally, try to remove the attitude roadblocks associated with making changes to the primary plan.

Summary

❑ The shorter, detailed planning horizon in the agile planning methodology makes mitigation less attractive than contingency planning.

❏ Contingency planning around scope and schedule risks is partially integrated into the overall agile project plan (network diagram) in the form of decision points and pathways.

❏ Weighting the many possible project pathways in an agile project is an effective way of prioritizing them, so that you can extend your detailed planning along a particular pathway, if necessary.

❏ An environment that implicitly views changes in the primary project plan as negative creates inherent delays in dealing with the issues that prompted the changes.

❏ Project course changes should be expected in the agile environment.

Risk Management Workflow

Risk management should be initiated during the tail end of the project planning process, and it should be reassessed periodically throughout the project. There are many benefits to employing a risk management process. They include setting realistic project expectations by maintaining visibility of risks, quicker recovery of problems through previously conceived contingency plans, and lower impact of potential problems through preventive actions. There are four basic parts to the risk management process:

1. Identify potential risks.
2. Assess the risks.
3. Make plans to address the risks.
4. Reassess the risks throughout the project.

This process is used in conjunction with the risk planning template. An electronic copy of this workflow and template can be downloaded from www.xocp.com.

Definition of Risk

Risk

A risk is an unplanned future event that may positively or negatively affect your project. Overall risk is usually quantified as impact times probability. There are also various qualitative adjustment factors that can be used when evaluating risk.

$$Risk = (Impact \text{ x } Probability) + Adjustment(s)$$

While risks are unplanned, they are not necessarily unanticipated. For instance, in the agile network planning approach, you may create a primary pathway, but anticipate events that could occur that would cause deviation from this path. These anticipated events (risks) are reflected as alternate pathways in the network diagram.

A risk is something that may happen in the future. Once the risk actually happens, it becomes an issue and should be addressed appropriately, usually through a contingency plan.

Risks versus issues

Risks are forward looking, while issues are events happening in real time. A risk may, and often does, turn into an issue. However, project managers (PMs) should strive not to let this happen. While the risk event is not officially planned (as part of your WBS and Gantt chart) it has been identified. How else would you know about it? Once identified, PMs should create contingency plans for the risk (i.e., alternate pathways). If this is done, then, when the risk event does happen, it does not turn into an issue. Rather, it triggers the contingency plan, which should address the unplanned risk event.

Identify the Risks

Review project planning outputs	During the initial project planning effort, you may encounter potential problems with the work breakdown structure (WBS), duration estimates, resource estimates, dependencies, constraints, etc. These should be noted and added to the project risk list.
Review project dependencies	Almost all project plans have some dependencies. Review these dependencies and determine if they pose a risk. If yes, then add them to the project risk list. For instance, your staffing may be dependent on the completion of another project (the engineers that you require will be moved to your project when their current project ends next month). Depending on the status and progress of that other project, this dependency may or may not qualify as a project risk.
Unknowns	During the initial project planning effort, you may encounter gaps for which you cannot obtain the necessary information. These gaps or unknowns should be added to the project risk list. For example, if you and your team cannot complete all sections of the project data sheet (PDS), then any omission should be noted as a project risk. The PDS is designed to only include the few core elements required before starting a project. If you are missing one of these core elements, you are at risk.
Lessons learned	Review the lessons learned from previous similar projects. First, try to address these in your project plan. If you cannot address them appropriately, they should be added to your project risk list.
Brainstorming	Identify people with experience on similar projects and lead individual or group brainstorming sessions focused on risk identification. You may start with your current project risk list and ask people to help identify additional potential failures around project schedule, scope, or resources.

Assess the Risks

Risk description	Create a summary description for each item on your project risk list. In many cases, it may be obvious what the risk means, based on the name you have given it on the project risk list. In other cases, it may not. In these latter cases, a brief description will go a long way toward minimizing confusion about the risk. The description should include the potential outcome should the risk occur (see next section). Also, by writing a brief description, you are forced to thoroughly think through the risk, so that you fully understand it. Often people combine two risks into one on the project risk list. Then, when they try to put a description together, they realize that they are dealing with two separate risks. Enter this information in the description and outcomes column of the risk template.
Risk outcome	Based on your description, determine what will probably happen if the risk event should occur. There are often multiple, possible scenarios that might occur, and, if so, they all should be captured as potential outcomes. Note: The outcome is different from the impact. Outcomes describe qualitatively what will happen because of the risk, while impact describes quantitatively the severity of the risk. (See the *risk impact* section below.) Enter this information in the description and outcomes column of the risk template.
Risk impact	For each item on your project risk list, determine the impact to the project if the risk event should occur. You can use rating scales (e.g., High-Medium-Low or a 1–10 scale) to rate the severity of the risk to the project in terms of its effect on project success. The rating should be determined by a group of knowledgeable people who are (ideally) part of the team. Enter this information in the impact column of the risk table.
Risk probability	For each item on your project risk list, determine the probability that the risk will actually occur. Again, you can use rating scales (e.g., High-Medium-Low or 1–10) to rate the probability of occurrence. Enter this information in the probability column of the risk template.
Risk detection (adjustment)	Since the basic $R = I \times P$ model can't possible capture all of the nuances of a particular project situation, it is

common to add a qualitative adjustment factor to the risk ordering. *Detection* is a good adjustment factor. Essentially, you want to determine if advance detection of the risk will be easy, hard, or, perhaps, impossible. Using detection as an adjustment factor may also have the side benefit of helping you devise specific detection mechanisms to use during project execution. I like to use a −1, 0, +1 adjustment, but you could use 1–10 or another scale also. If you use detection as a risk-quantifying factor, the equation becomes:

$$Risk = Impact \times Probability + Detection\ Adj.$$

Note: This step is optional. Enter this information in the detection adjustment column of the risk template.

| Qualitative adjustments | The most efficient and effective adjustment often just uses professional judgment (brainstorming with your core team) to determine an adjustment. During this process, keep in mind that you need to find the High-High or High-Medium risks first. The primary goal here is to add or subtract points to break ties in the overall risk score so that a clearer prioritization can be determined. Stay focused on the top part of your list until you are comfortable with the relative ordering, then you can move on to bottom of the list. You should use the same scale as for the detection adjustment (i.e. −1, 0, +1). If you use a qualitative risk adjustment factor, the equation becomes:

$$Risk = Impact \times Probability + Detection\ Adj. + Qualitative\ Adj.$$

Note: This step is optional. Enter this information in the qualitative adjustment column of the risk template. |
| Prioritization | As mentioned previously, overall risk is usually quantified as impact times probability (I × P) plus adjustment factors. Based on your team's assessment of each risk's impact, probability, and adjustments, you should be able to put them in rank order with the High Impact, High Probability risks at the top. I suggest that you don't spend a lot of time trying to get the bottom half of the list in exact priority order. There are more quantitative risk models that can be used to get a better ordering, but they |

require more inputs. This simplistic model will usually
identify the big risks pretty well.

Order the risks in the risk table from highest to lowest (top to bottom).

Make Plans to Address the Risks

Identify risks to manage	Since you can only spend so much time focused on risks, you need to determine which ones you will manage and which ones you won't. This is usually the same as the top-priority risks that you previously identified, but not always. For example, it may be very easy to address some low-priority risks, so you decide to take care of them. It may be incredibly difficult to address a high-priority risk, so you determine that it is not worth spending the energy to address it. Whether or not a risk is addressed should be a conscious decision by the PM. By not addressing an identified risk you are, in fact, accepting it. PMs should document all risks that are accepted so that it does not appear that they were merely forgotten or missed all together. Indicate acceptance of a risk in the mitigation/contingency plan section of the risk template.
Mitigation plans	Mitigation can be thought of as doing extra project work in an effort to prevent the risk event from occurring. This is an effective way to address a risk, assuming the benefits (of preventing the risk) outweigh the added costs of the mitigation. Crafting a mitigation involves understanding the root cause of the risk, brainstorming potential ways to prevent the risk, and then breaking them down into WBS elements and individual tasks that can be added to the detailed project plan. When optimizing your overall project schedule, mitigation plans often end up on the chopping block as a way to save time and resources. By eliminating a valid mitigation plan, you are essentially accepting the risk, or taking a gamble that the risk will not occur. You may win, or you may lose. This is okay, but again, it should be a conscious PM decision weighed against other possible optimization alternatives. Describe any mitigation plans in the mitigation/contingency section of the risk template.

Contingency plans	Contingency plans are subsets of the overall project plans that only get used if the specific risk event does occur. The objective of a contingency plan is to rapidly neutralize the impact of a risk event on your project. Contingency plans should be created using the same process and thought that goes into creating any project plan. Contingency plans for high-priority risks can be just as important as the primary project plan. After your overall project plan has been optimized, identify your top-priority risks that do not have mitigation plans. You should create contingency plans for these risks. Also, if you have any high-priority risks with mitigation plans, but you are still uncertain of their potential success, then these should also have contingency plans. Describe any contingency plans in the mitigation/ contingency section of the risk template, and depict the contingency as an alternate pathway on the project network diagram.
Triggers	Identify a triggering event for each contingency-managed risk. Once the trigger occurs, the contingency plan is initiated. Like a detection event, triggering events should be watched for by the PM during the project execution.

Reassess the Risks During the Project Execution

Top risk list	Maintain a current list of the highest-priority risks and distribute it with your regular project status reports (see Appendix A for an example of a Project Status Reporting template and workflow). Use this list as a means to regularly communicate top risks, their consequences, and the current mitigation/contingency strategy. This is an excellent way to keep risks visible to the team and management so that they are not forgotten. It also tends to keep people thinking of new and better ways to address the risks. A mitigation or contingency plan that was not obvious at the start may become apparent midway through the project.
Periodic review	Once a quarter is usually a good schedule to set for formally reviewing your project risks in detail. However, you should determine a period that is appropriate for your project. Use the same basic process described in this document, with the exception of eliminating risks that are associated with activities that have already been completed.

Integration

Status reporting	A summary of the top risks captured in this process should be integrated into the project's periodic status reports.
Action items	A risk is not a task or an action item. However, as part of your mitigation or contingency plan, one or more action items or tasks may be assigned. These should be added to the project Gantt chart or action item list. The over-reaching risk should remain on this list. Specific cross-references can be tagged on the Gantt chart, action items list, and risk list, if desired.

Template for Risk Planning

[Project Name] Risks

Risk description and potential outcome	Impact (H-M-L)	Probability (H-M-L)	Detection adjustment (−1, 0, +1)	Qualitative adjustment (−1, 0, +1)	Description of mitigation/ contingency plan and triggers
Risk #1	M	H		−1	Enter description here.
Risk #2	M	L		0	Enter description here.

9

MANAGEMENT: CREATING AN ENVIRONMENT OF AGILITY

Agile project management is about deftly managing the change in requirements associated with project uncertainty, so that it becomes a positive force for both the project and the business, rather than a negative one. The project manager guides the team through the changes necessary to bring the project to a successful completion. The individual team members execute the activities that bring about successful course changes. Now, it is up to management to create an environment that will nourish the seeds of change and creativity, rather than crushing or stifling them.

Creating an environment that is supportive of change is not easy, especially when you consider that management must balance the project needs against the longer-term business planning needs, which are generally rooted in predictability. The stability and certainty, which is so often strived for in classic project management, is a perfect match for long-term business planning. Replacing that predictability with the controlled chaos of the agile project can be unnerving for most managers. Yet, continuing to employ classic methods in an agile environment will likely result in the same loss of predictability—and perhaps something worse.

When discussing change from the management perspective, we need to cover two dimensions. First, we must look at the dimension of change within the actual project. An agile project is more likely to take a zigzag course through a network of pathways to reach its completion point. By contrast, a classic project may take a more direct route along a well-planned primary path. The second dimension to examine is the organizational change that must come about to support the agile project. This dimension includes redefining individual, leadership, and organizational roles to meet the dynamic needs of the project, and it is definitely more difficult to address. We should also draw a distinction between senior management and functional management. While in some cases these two types of management overlap and may actually be the same, for the purposes of this discussion, we'll use the following broad definitions to reflect the matrix organization used by most companies:

❑ *Executive or upper managers* are those people who create the long-term business strategy and direction for the overall organization.

❑ *Functional managers* are those people who manage a specific part of an organization made up of people of similar skills sets (e.g., R&D, marketing, or manufacturing). These managers loan out their resources to projects, based on their particular needs.

Upper Management and Project Change

In the classic project environment, upper management has minimal involvement with course changes within a project. Their primary project roles include endorsing/sponsoring the project, committing resources, setting a project deadline, receiving status reports, managing escalations, and providing rewards to motivate the team. Perhaps upper management's only direct involvement in managing project change might be in approving an unexpected course change before implementation, or encouraging the team to "try something new." Generally, upper management does not get actively involved in steering the project.

In the very fluid world of the agile project, the role of upper management (see Figure 9-1) becomes more active, and not just on the back end by approving changes, but on the front end, influencing

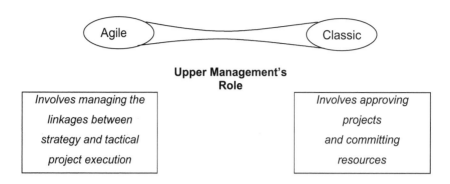

Figure 9-1. Upper management's role in the agile versus classic project.

them. Upper management is largely concerned with fulfilling business strategy (at least partially) through the successful execution of tactical projects. In a predictable business and technical environment, management would define a set of projects that, in total, would lead to the fulfillment of key business objectives or strategy. These projects would be handed off to various functional areas and cross-functional project managers for planning and execution. Since the projects were well defined and bounded, management could let them run independently and would only need to check on their status periodically.

On the other hand, an uncertain, fast-changing business environment requires that the business strategy be tightly linked to the tactical projects during execution, as well as in definition, so that each exerts the appropriate influence on the other (see Figure 9-2). Upper management's role shifts to one of understanding the linkages between the business planning process, business strategy, project portfolio, and tactical projects, then facilitating course change decisions based on their knowledge of the high-level business environment.

Each of these dimensions (business strategy, business objectives, programs, and projects) may be owned by a different person in the organization. Since there is some ripple effect that ties them all to-

Agile Strategy

Understand and manage the linkages between business strategy, high-level objectives, and the tactical project portfolio to better keep your organization on task to achieve its high-level strategies.

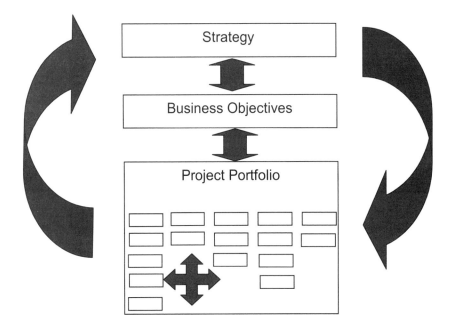

Figure 9-2. Strategy, business objectives, and tactical projects all exert appropriate influences on each other.

gether, it is critical that the owners of each of these dimensions know where they fit in. Generally, a big, upstream change (i.e., a strategy change) will have a greater ripple affect on the downstream areas like the tactical projects, but not always. In the agile world, everything is a project, and whole business strategies may hinge on the outcomes of a few key projects. In a nutshell, there can be a two-way ripple effect. The more you understand how what you're doing may affect someone else, as well as how what they're doing will affect you, the better.

In the agile paradigm, senior management must be more actively involved in understanding project-level decisions, since the ripples caused by these decisions can potentially impact the high-level strategy. Likewise, their strategy-level decisions have potentially magnified downstream impacts; thus, they need to understand how changes in the business strategy may impact a specific project, or all portfolio projects in general, before enacting anything at the high level. In this way, they can avoid adverse downstream consequences that would delay rather than accelerate any desired strategy-level change. I wouldn't think that upper management needs to be intimately up-to-date with all project interactions; however, it should expect to be pulled into the project-level decision-making process more often in the agile environment than the classic one.

In the agile project environment, there is a two-way ripple effect between the high-level business strategy and the tactical project portfolio when either of them change.

Functional Management and Project Change

The functional manager really has two project-related roles in the classic, matrix management model. First, she is responsible for hiring (and then developing) personnel within her area with the intent of building the necessary skills to advance overall functional capabilities. Second, she allocates personnel, as needed, to work on various projects. This setup, in a way, isolates the functional manager from direct involvement in the project. Any project information relayed to her, or any influence exerted by her on the project, is conveyed via the people that she has allocated to the project.

In the agile environment, the functional manager must become more directly involved with the project than she is in the classic project environment. In keeping with our concept of aligning the business and projects, the functional manager must keep her organization aligned with both. For projects, this means obtaining the people with those critical skills needed for project success in the agile environment. These skills include the ability to work across traditional functional boundaries, as well as the ability to perform detailed technical tasks. Because of the rapid pace of change in agile projects, the functional manager must know when to hire a permanent employee and when the use of a consultant, or temporary employee, would be better. Hiring in today's business environment is a big commitment. It must be handled appropriately to support both the company and project objectives. The only way to do this effectively is to work directly with the project managers so that you know the project objectives, direction, and required skill sets. In essence, the functional manager is now being asked to obtain and develop project-specific skills rather than the more general, functional skills.

Agile Strategy

Get more directly involved with projects so that you can provide the right personnel/skills to advance them, and thus advance the overall organization.

How people with these skills are acquired can have a profound positive or negative influence itself on the business. For instance, if you need someone to provide high-level technical direction, as well as to form the cross-boundary networks necessary to nourish new ideas, then it's more desirable to add this person permanently to your core team. Even after this particular project is over, a person with these uncommon skills can surely contribute to the next one. In the agile project environment, the bigger change involves the greater use of consultants for specific technical roles. There are two reasons that agile businesses should not be spending their energy and money trying to develop permanent, specific, technical skill sets. First, the very nature of the agile environment means that the need for that specific skill could vanish overnight, if the project takes an unexpected turn. This creates risk for the business, in the form of an unwanted liability (i.e., person). And second, agile projects often need specific skills for short periods of time, or on an as-needed basis. In these cases, it doesn't make sense to hire a full-time person, even if you want to. As an alternative, you could have one of your permanent employees take on a task that's outside of her specific expertise. This approach is good for personnel development but bad for the agile project, since it will not get the high-level expertise that's needed. Generally, it's more efficient for the project (and the company in the long run) to outsource these roles to experts, even at a premium.

Agile Strategy

Look to outsourcing as a means of acquiring specific technical talent, especially if this talent can't be repurposed, in the event that the project in question no longer needs it.

Upper Management and Organizational Change

Organizational change is a totally different animal from project change. People rationalize that project change is temporary and, therefore, "worth a try" to see if it really works. Organizational change, on the other hand, is perceived as a more permanent modification in the way we do our jobs, so people generally feel threatened by organizational change. This is even more the case when the change is driven by the project team (rather than by management). In this new and ever-changing economy, the natural tendency of people is still to resist organizational change.

Because projects are themselves instruments of change, they are on the forefront of the organizational evolution. By the very nature of the change they try to accomplish, project teams push the organizational envelope, constantly discovering new organizational issues to address. As these new organizational challenges are uncovered, one of two things may happen. First, the organization can adapt and reinvent itself to meet the needs of the project. Or, second, the organization will refuse to yield, and it will force the project team to work within the current organizational framework. Depending on the situation, either one of these actions may be appropriate.

In the case of the truly agile project, one breaking new ground that is fraught with uncertainty, the first option is the one of choice. As discussed in Chapter 3, the project becomes the business in the agile environment. There is little precedent to work from and, therefore, little reason to hold to strict organizational barriers. The organization, driven by the needs of the project, needs to morph itself into a support mechanism to facilitate project progress. All too often, functional organizations put their needs ahead of the project's needs for purely parochial reasons. This silo mentality is a killer of agile projects.

It is in these situations that management must create an environment that is supportive and encourages organizational reinvention. This includes both rebalancing the matrix to divide responsibilities differently, as well as looking at new ways of doing work. Inevitably, it means crossing over and blurring traditional functional boundaries, which is, in fact, a key dynamic in the agile project. The agile project is a mechanism that is trying to create something never created before. An agile organization that can reinvent itself to support the agile project is a critical enabler of project success.

Agile Strategy

Create an environment that enables the breakdown and reinvention of traditional functional boundaries, if so required by the project and the business.

In the case of an operational business, such as a customer support call center, it is necessary to have great efficiencies across both staff and processes. A project to set up a new family of products for customer support must mesh smoothly with the current processes. Usually, these types of systems have been honed to great efficiency over several years of incremental improvements. In these cases, it does not make sense to reinvent the organization around the project. Instead, you should be looking at how to make the project fit the processes. (Note that these are not necessarily agile projects.)

The two examples of organizational adaptability (cited above and summarized in Figure 9-3) represent opposite extremes, making the contrast easy to see. As a champion of change, project managers need to help other stakeholders see the different needs of various projects and organizations, then highlight the gaps. Most organizations that resist change do not understand the context or need for the change, so they are also not necessarily motivated to support an organizational

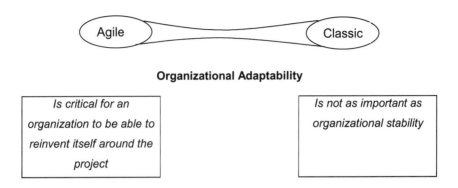

Figure 9-3. Organizational adaptability in an agile versus classic PM environment.

change. It is the job of the project manager to make the argument for organizational change, and the job of senior management to put in place mechanisms that motivate functional management to support the necessary changes.

Functional Management and Organizational Change

The functional management level is where organizational change efforts are solidified or circumvented. While senior managers are charged with creating an atmosphere conducive to organizational change, it is the functional managers who must make it happen. Whereas senior management generally represents high-level goals for the organization, functional management usually has more specific goals that don't always completely align with those of the project. Additionally, most organizations have competitive undercurrents between departments and functional areas. A certain amount of organizational competition or tension is actually healthy for the business. It forces people to continually push themselves toward improvement. However, all too often the tension becomes personal when people become protective of their turf and not only fend off others who might encroach on them, but actively try to expand their area of influence. This line of thinking is the basis of the so-called silo mentality, where strengthening of the silo becomes more important than the overall organizational goals to the functional manager. This attitude naturally is filtered down to the individuals who work on the project teams, and this is where the problem is generally first identified.

As the agile project progresses, it is not only breaking new ground within the project itself, but it is also breaking new organizational ground. The project manager and other change champions will be looking for ways to bridge these new organizational obstacles. Both the project team and the functional management team must work together to address these never-before-addressed organizational challenges (see Figure 9-4). Usually, it will be the project team that pushes for change, since its members have identified it as a potential issue preventing the project from moving forward. On the other hand, functional management may be somewhat resistant to change, since it's looking for more predictability and less risk within its domain. Functional managers generally don't see the whole picture from the project's perspective, and, very often, the project team doesn't spend the time to educate them. Many functional managers have been brought up in the old school, where project teams operated within already-defined organizational boundaries, not the other way around. The change champions of the project team need to spend time making their case to functional managers also. They must lay out the big picture and explain why the rapid pace of change in today's business environment requires increased organizational agility. They must show how participating in the creation of this organizational agility

	Project Change	Organizational Change
Upper Management	Manages the linkages between the business strategy and the tactical project portfolio	Creates an environment supportive of organizational change
Functional Management	Obtains and aligns the skills necessary to advance projects	Works with project teams to design and implement organizational changes

Figure 9-4. A summary of management roles unique to the agile project environment.

will actually strengthen, not weaken, each manager's respective functional organization.

Agile Strategy

Make the case to management regarding organizational change by laying out the big picture and its implications to the project, the functional areas, and the overall business.

The leadership organizations of the future will be those with the capacity and agility to adapt to the situation at hand and effectively execute strategy through projects. Whether at the business level or the department level, organizations that cannot, or will not, adapt will be left behind and may eventually be dismantled in favor of more flexible structures.

Summary

- ❑ Senior management must understand the linkages between business planning, portfolio management, and tactical project execution.
- ❑ In the agile project environment, there is a two-way ripple effect between the high-level business strategy and the tactical project portfolio when either of them changes.
- ❑ Functional managers should consider outsourcing as a means to staff agile projects, more so than for classic ones.
- ❑ Agile project teams constantly push the organizational envelope and uncover new organizational obstacles to overcome.
- ❑ The capability of an organization to reinvent itself is an enabler of agile PM, as well as overall organizational agility.
- ❑ The silo mentality is a killer of organizational reinvention.
- ❑ Laying out the big picture of the agile project will help all levels of management understand the need for organizational reinvention.

10

THE OPERATIONAL PROJECT MANAGEMENT INFRASTRUCTURE

This chapter touches on the unglamorous parts of successful project management. It provides some practical organization to topics that you are largely familiar with, but perhaps never thought were important enough to develop further or standardize in your company. Hopefully, you will see that there is some low-hanging fruit and that picking it is not only easy, but will have a dramatic affect on your project management agility.

Developing a project management infrastructure is one of those *important* but not necessarily *urgent* internal activities that organizations must undertake to support their project managers. It is important because with a well-honed and integrated set of tools and processes at his disposal, the project manager is freed up from administrative PM duties and can focus on some of the more critical duties discussed in Chapter 5. Unfortunately, for many organizations, PM infrastructure development is just not urgent enough to make it to the top of their list. Ironically, this is because most project managers are able to "get by" using their own homemade systems, which are usually based on multiple different general-purpose software programs. So, while the inherent organizational capabilities of project managers enable them to move forward despite a lack of specialized PM tools, they are forced to work on lower-value administrative areas of PM. Consequently, the organization itself never reaps the full return from its investment in project management.

What Exactly Is an Operational Project Management Infrastructure, and Why Do I Need One?

A project management infrastructure is an organized set of tools and processes that can facilitate the project management process from start to finish. While these tools and processes are usually clumped together, I find that it makes more sense to categorize them into two broad groups (see Figure 10-1). The first grouping applies to the "initiation and planning" processes. The second is those tools and processes that apply to "execution and control." This chapter is primarily focused on the second group, which is where agile projects can gain the most benefits; however, as you will see, there is some overlap.

I use the term *operational* because we are dealing with those tools, processes, and systems that facilitate day-to-day project management activities rather than those tasks that generally take place on a more periodic basis, such as planning. I use the term *infrastructure* to mean that the tools and processes in question are organized and integrated

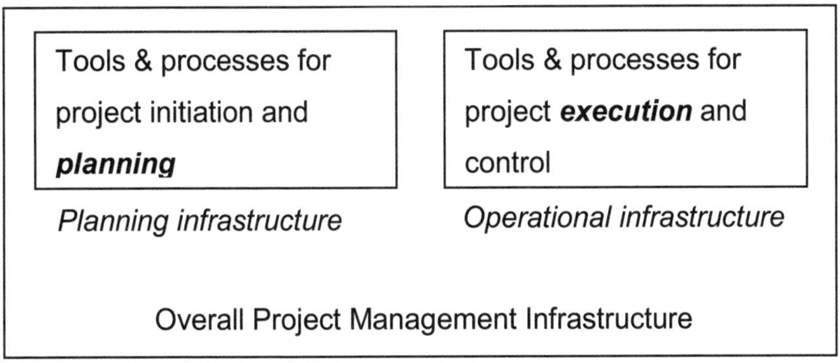

Tools & processes for project initiation and *planning*	Tools & processes for project *execution* and control
Planning infrastructure	*Operational infrastructure*
Overall Project Management Infrastructure	

Figure 10-1. Project management infrastructures are focused in two broad areas, planning and execution.

in a logical manner, as opposed to merely being a collection of things with no cohesive thread holding them together. The relationship between these elements and project management is shown in Figure 10-2.

Agile Strategy

Create an operational project management infrastructure to help your project managers efficiently manage day-to-day PM activities such as task, action item, issue, and communications management.

All projects require some type of operational infrastructure to operate efficiently. The team needs to know how progress will be tracked and reported, how communications will be managed, how information will be shared, and how changes will be handled. These tools and processes collectively support the project manager in managing the project. An example of an operational project management infrastructure is given at the end of this chapter.

To further illustrate this point, here's another example. Let's say a new project manager is hired from the outside or internally transfers from another type of job. One of the first questions she will probably ask is: "How do you guys manage projects?" It's not that she doesn't know how to do the job; rather, she wants to know if there are methods and tools in place that have been used effectively in the past. After all, why should she reinvent the wheel if she doesn't have to? Additionally, she will want to use tools that are consistent with what other project managers use, so team members who contribute to multiple teams won't be confused.

You may be surprised, but in all but the most mature project man-

Figure 10-2. The operational project management infrastructure.

agement organizations (or those that have purchased a sophisticated enterprise software solution), there is generally no consistent operational infrastructure that is driven by the company. And, as you may suspect, most mature project management organizations tend to be in large conventional companies. The sheer volume and complexity of projects that large organizations undertake usually justifies the investment of time and resources necessary to develop both a planning and operational infrastructure for managing projects. On the other hand, there is a perception that smaller, faster-moving companies do not really need formal project management at all, let alone an operational infrastructure, because their projects aren't as large or complex.

This line of thinking is fundamentally flawed because it only looks at project size or volume of projects as the justifications to develop a consistent infrastructure and does not consider the effects of uncertainty on project execution. The uncertainty of the agile environment creates frequent changes and therefore generates many action items, issues, and risks that don't appear on the initial project plan. Managing these additional elements, as well as the increased communications, is as critical to project success as managing those identified in the original plan. Without an organized process for keeping these elements tied to the primary plan, your project can quickly go off-course.

Agile Strategy

Ensure that your operational infrastructure integrates the status of unplanned action items and issues with those of the original project plan, to deftly manage the frequent and rapid changes to that plan.

The Agile Infrastructure

It's no wonder that in the more classically designed project management offices (PMOs), there is more emphasis on tools and processes associated with the planning phase than the execution phase. These companies fully expect that they will be able to develop a robust upfront plan and then follow it closely for the duration of the project.

Agile projects are quite the opposite (see Figure 10-3). Project managers expect their initial plan to change at some point, so they spend less effort on detailed planning at the start of the project and more effort on managing the inevitable changes. Obviously, there still has to be a reasonable planning element in the agile environment, just not as detailed as in the classic environment. This partially explains why it can be frustrating to use some of the common project management software tools on the market today—they are designed for detailed up-front planning, but do not help much with managing the many "unplanned" action items that pop up during project execution.

Agile Strategy

When selecting project management tools, pick those that facilitate tasks associated with executing the project. You want the ability to easily integrate elements such as action items and issue management into the project timeline to assess their effect on the overall project.

Perils of On-the-Fly Process Development

When no standard operational infrastructure is available, project managers usually create their own tools and processes "on the fly" to manage the project at hand. They probably have some minimal level of

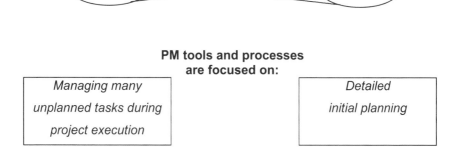

Figure 10-3. The focus of PM tools in an agile versus classic environment.

discussion and/or training for their team members to acclimate them to the tools and to avoid confusion. Once the project is completed, the team disbands and people go on to other projects and the process repeats. Best practices may travel with individuals but are generally not pervasive. Furthermore, the ad hoc tools and processes created are usually incomplete and nearly always inconsistent from project manager to project manager. This, in turn, can lead to inefficiencies and frustration on project teams.

Infrastructure may include a wide range of processes, practices, software tools, templates, and forms. These elements are critical to effective and agile project management, so skilled resources need to be allocated to develop and support them. Agile organizations tend to have a culture of continual learning. With each new project, you probably learn something that will strengthen a particular piece of the infrastructure. Without resources committed to maintaining the infrastructure, these potential improvement ideas will be lost. The paradox is that "process development" resources are much less likely to be available to the agile organization, since we are usually talking about a smaller and leaner organization. Yet this is exactly where these resources can add enormous value.

Forcing the project team, rather than dedicated process development resources, to invent the infrastructure will likely have a negative effect on the project execution. It can also produce a suboptimal infrastructure. First, the team would usually have to do this work concurrently with executing the project, which takes time away from actual project tasks, in turn slowing the project. Second, the project manager and team are not necessarily process development experts. They may design processes that are inefficient, only work for specific situations, or are not cleanly integrated, which can lead to any number of problems down the road, thus reducing agility in terms of speed and making decisions correctly. Third, the project manager and team may not view these activities as part of their job, so they may decide to omit certain tools and processes completely and just "wing" it. When this happens, the implications are the same as mentioned previously: inconsistencies, inefficiencies, and possibly frustration.

Agile Strategy

Allocate specialized resources/expertise to develop and maintain your project management infrastructure and you will accelerate your progress toward PM agility.

The overall goal is that the organization have the basic operational infrastructure in place, then the team can build on or modify it as necessary for specific situations. By employing dedicated expertise to facilitate these improvements, the project-specific modifications will, over time, become fewer and fewer. At that point, you will have developed a consistent and effective operational infrastructure, tuned to your unique business environment, and truly gained ground in your quest for agility.

Infrastructure As a Facilitator of Communications

An additional, significant value-add of an operational infrastructure is that problems, miscommunications, and other conflicts can be avoided during the project. The infrastructure lays out the details of how the project will be managed, thus leaving little to guesswork. Without an established operational infrastructure, team members who are not familiar with each other may be timid to ask basic questions such as "How will the project be managed?" because they think that everyone already knows. That's a recipe for confusion and inefficiency. Much of the infrastructure should be referenced in the project communications plan (see Chapter 4). Any disagreement can then be discussed and resolved directly rather than indirectly, which will help to head off many team dynamics issues.

An integrated operational infrastructure is also a very efficient way to capture and distribute critical project information to the various stakeholders (e.g., management, project managers/leaders, contributors) through various reporting mechanisms. This is especially true for a program or portfolio that is composed of many individual but linked projects. A change in one project or environmental variable may have a ripple effect on several other projects. Likewise, a shift in high-level strategy or functional direction could have a similar ripple effect through various projects. A good operational infrastructure helps to efficiently propagate all relevant information and changes to the appropriate parties.

Teams are usually aligned with major projects; however, in an agile environment, a working team can also be a small group that is quickly brought together to solve a particular issue and later disbanded, a functional group working on process improvement activities within that function, or a management team dealing with a competitive threat. The efforts of these teams, while not formally defined as a "project," can be captured and analyzed along with other PM efforts as part of the infrastructure.

The operational PM infrastructure is like a machine that takes in real-time project data from many sources, analyzes it, and then creates valuable information for the project teams to use in making decisions and running the projects. The inputs to this machine may be documents, online tools, e-mails, or voice mails and may include meeting minutes, decisions, issues, action items, risks, status reports, and anything else related to the project. While this will definitely take some effort on the part of the team members, the system should be designed to make input of the data as painless as possible. The basic value proposition of the PM infrastructure should be that the effort required to provide input to the machine (i.e., the infrastructure) will pay off many times in the form of robust information on which project and business decisions can be based.

Agile Infrastructure As a Means to Reduce Administrative Headaches

A final benefit of a well-designed operational infrastructure is that it can greatly facilitate the administrative parts of managing a project. This benefit is largely related to efficiency, but can also be somewhat of a motivator for the project manager. Much of successful project

management is about paying close attention to detail around administrative tasks, such as documentation, status reporting, action item
follow-up, activity synchronization, issue management, and project
timeline updating. Project managers sometimes employ as many as
three to four separate software packages to handle administrative functions. The challenge is to keep all of the information integrated and
up-to-date. While they are not impossible tasks, these cumbersome
administrative duties are relatively distasteful to most professionals,
who would rather focus on higher-level contributions.

Furthermore, these administrative tasks tend to be proportional to
the level of uncertainty, making them increasingly more time-consuming
in the agile project. Issues may arise, the project may fall behind
schedule, action items are assigned, or something outside the project
may occur that will affect the team. Very soon the administrative effort
to keep all of these events organized and prioritized becomes daunt-
ing. This is especially true if you are using multiple software tools that
are only integrated through your own transcription or by using copy-
and-paste techniques. In this scenario, it is not unrealistic for the project manager to get sucked further into a black hole of administrative
activities, which in turn can be quite demotivating.

However, both the administrative and motivational issues can be
addressed by a robust operational infrastructure. For example, let's say
that on route to a major milestone, the team encounters a technical
obstacle. To overcome this challenge, resources are pulled from other
current activities, effectively stopping them, and multiple subteams are
formed to attack the problem. These subteams start work immediately
on brainstorming an approach to the problem, but not necessarily a
detailed schedule. Nonetheless, many action items get assigned and
the team members disperse to start work. This should be an exciting
time for the project manager, during which she adds significant value
to the project. However, all too often the project manager spends her
time running around documenting and following up on these action
items and creating timelines and status reports, all the while hoping
that there is some coordination of the major efforts. With an operational infrastructure in place, these administrative tasks would be handled much more efficiently, thus freeing up the project manager to get

out in front of the team to direct traffic, which is where she prefers to be in the first place.

Implementing Your Agile Infrastructure

Many organizations tend to build their project management infrastructure around available software rather than first figuring out their processes manually. This often comes down to economics, since it is generally very expensive to have custom software written around your unique processes. However, when you are developing an agile infrastructure, this can be a dangerous trap because many of the popular off-the-shelf tools have been developed and optimized around the classic PM environment, so they emphasize front-end activities, like planning and budgeting, instead of execution. Newer tools are more configurable and include functions that automate the execution of projects. However, these enterprise-level tools tend to be prohibitively expensive for smaller agile businesses. The list below outlines some basic considerations when selecting PM software. I prefer tools that do a good job of covering the basics while leaving out the bells and whistles, which are often costly, have few actual applications, and make the tools difficult to use. Ease of use is one of those characteristics that doesn't get much attention when evaluating software, yet is incredibly important for the simple reason that if the software is hard to use, it won't get used.

Agile Strategy

Select software tools that cover the basics well, leave out the bells and whistles, and are easy to use.

Since agile project management concepts are still in their infancy, it may make more sense to manually design an infrastructure tailored to your specific needs and ease into integrated software solutions as ones that meet your needs and budget become available. While, as a rule, I believe that working with multiple distinct software packages

Considerations for Selecting PM Software Tools for the Agile Project Environment

1. Does the software help with execution-stage activities, such as action item and issue management, as well as planning-stage activities like Gantt chart creation?

2. Does it facilitate administrative duties by integrating key project information? Examples of commonly integrated elements include:
   - ❏ Timeline
   - ❏ Action items
   - ❏ Issues
   - ❏ Risks
   - ❏ Status reporting

3. Does it create reports in a format that can be viewed with standard office tools? (Reports generated in standard formats are easier to share and therefore facilitate communications.)

4. Does it create network diagrams?

5. Does it do top-down and bottom-up estimating?

6. Does it have powerful features that you'll probably never use? You'll have to pay for these features, even if they are not relevant to your needs.

7. Is the cost of the software in line with your budget? Consider that you may need to purchase several copies or a site license (for project managers and team members).

8. Is it easy to use? If the program is hard to use, it won't get used.

---

is cumbersome and inefficient, this may be the best option for developing your initial operational infrastructure. This approach also gives you the opportunity to work the bugs out of your processes before investing in more expensive, integrated systems. At the end of this chapter, you'll find a high-level example of what an operational infrastructure may look like. Hopefully, it will spark some thoughts on how you might implement your own infrastructure manually (using multiple general-purpose and disconnected software programs, as opposed to specialized and integrated PM software solutions).

Manual implementation of an operational infrastructure is a viable, cost-effective, and logical way to get started in this area. However, there are a few keys to success in a manual implementation and they revolve around the project management organization itself—specifically, how PM duties are divided up. Most companies don't differentiate how duties are split among different PM roles. They have only a single set of duties, which is "do everything." They may have different levels of PM responsibility, such as junior or senior project manager, which is related to the importance or complexity of assignments, but the basic duties are the same.

The effective implementation of a manual operational infrastructure requires organizations to create three distinct PM roles that work together to increase the overall value of the project management office. These roles are:

❑ *Process Developer.* This is the person who actually develops the detailed tools, processes, and templates, as well as designs how they will work together. The architecture at the end of this chapter, along with the workflows throughout the book, will give your process expert a start in this area. However, she will still want to do some customization for your unique project/business environment and, just as important, will need to maintain the infrastructure as it evolves.

❑ *Program Analyst.* This person is an expert user of the tools and processes that make up the infrastructure. This individual is skilled in using the tools not only for routine tracking and maintenance tasks, but also for more crucial analysis tasks. Note that basic analysis tools should already be designed and built into the infrastructure's tracking and reporting mechanisms. This role is especially valuable when there are multiple, related projects running independently. Ideally, a single program analyst will run the infrastructure for the whole organization and will support several project managers. Since the program analyst has the best view of the real-time project information coming in from the various projects, he is in the best position to identify and analyze potential interproject issues. The program analyst also creates various types of reports for communicating his analyses and other key project information to the project managers, team members, and other stakeholders in a timely fashion.

❑ *Project Manager.* With the previous two roles defined, the project manager doesn't have to develop or maintain tools and processes, become an expert user of tools, maintain detailed project data, or watch for low-level problems. She should be examining the environment external to the project (to ensure that the project remains aligned with core business objectives), facilitating the resolution of conflicts and issues (identified by the program analyst), managing communication with key stakeholders, performing other duties described in Chapter 5, and generally guiding the team and project forward.

Agile Strategy

Break up your project management duties into three distinct roles—the process developer, the program analyst, and the project manager—to both facilitate the operation of your project infrastructure and motivate your PM team.

Summary

- ❑ All projects need some type of operational infrastructure to operate efficiently.

- ❑ Agile projects need an infrastructure that's more focused on managing the execution phase of the project rather than the planning phase, which a majority of available software tools are geared toward.

- ❑ Project management infrastructure offloads administrative PM tasks from the project manager, thereby enabling him to focus on higher-level duties.

- ❑ Ideally, project management infrastructures should have specialized and dedicated resources allocated to develop, support, and operate them, including a process developer and program analyst. These resources are part of the umbrella project management office, but generally outside of any specific project team.

Sample Agile Project
Management Infrastructure

Figure 10-4 illustrates the architecture of an operational PM infrastructure. The operational PM infrastructure described here refers to a program (i.e., a group of related projects with common overall objectives), but it can be scaled back for a single project.

An integrated PM infrastructure is an efficient way to capture and distribute critical project information to various stakeholders (i.e., management, project managers/leaders, and contributors). This is especially true for agile programs that are composed of many individual but linked projects. A change in one project may have a ripple effect on several other projects. Likewise, a shift in high-level strategy or functional direction could also have a ripple effect through various individual projects. It is generally preferred to have a dedicated resource, such as a program analyst, to own the collection, analysis, and dissemination of information that flows through the operational infrastructure.

Operational PM Infrastructure Workflow

The following table describes a manual implementation of an operational PM infrastructure. The primary intent is to show how the major pieces of the PM infrastructure interact with each other to efficiently create the project information needed by management and project managers to drive programs forward. Detailed descriptions and instructions for individual PM tools/processes are available as separate documents, and the chapters where you can find them are cross-referenced.

An electronic copy of this process can be downloaded from www.xocp .com.

Working Teams

Overview

This section represents all of the *working teams* in an organization. *Working team* is defined to mean groups that are working on completing a given (i.e., part of a) project, whether large or small. In many cases, teams are aligned with projects. However, a working team can also be a small group that is quickly brought together to solve a particular issue and later disbanded, a functional group working on process improvement activities, or a management team dealing with steering the overall program.

There are two ways for project teams to get program

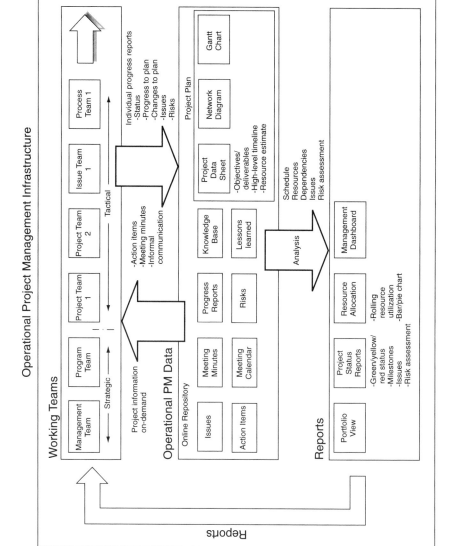

Figure 10-4. Architecture of an operational PM infrastructure.

information, on demand or via formal reports, which are discussed below.

Information on demand	Project information is often made available online via the Web or a shared drive. These repositories of project information can be accessed by team members on demand and, ideally, are managed by the Program Analyst. This is the best place to get real-time data and information since it should be updated continuously as new data flows in.
Reports	The second, and arguably more valuable, way that project stakeholders can receive project information is via reports. The Program Analyst is responsible for organizing and analyzing the project data and then generating certain regular reports, which are described below. The current report formats should be customized to meet the needs of individual team members.

Operational PM Data

Overview	This section is the main repository for project management data. Ultimately, this data is processed and analyzed (by the Program Analyst) with the objective of providing valuable support information to the various project managers to use in leading their projects. PM data may be generated and collected in many forms, including all of the elements described below.
Project Data Sheets (PDS)	See the *Project Data Sheet Template* and *Workflow* (Chapter 7) for details. Project Data Sheets are core elements in the operational PM infrastructure. These can be thought of as project executive summaries that are used to quickly and efficiently communicate the project "plan." Because they do not require extensive detail, they can be created with minimal effort by project leaders and/or project managers.
Gantt charts	These are detailed project timelines. While the Project Data Sheet describes the high-level project milestones, the Gantt chart contains the individual tasks leading up to each milestone, along with their respective characteristics such as owner, duration, dependencies, etc. Not all projects require detailed Gantt charts depending on the overall scope, but when applicable, they are a good way to think through the sequence of project details.

Network diagrams	See the *Project Data Sheet Template* and *Workflow* (Chapter 7) for details. Network diagrams provide a high-level view of the various project pathways and decision points and can be invaluable in guiding a project in an agile environment.
Action items	See the *Action Items Tracking Process* in Appendix C for details. These are the many tasks that get assigned during the project execution phase but do not make it onto the project Gantt chart. It is critical to stay on top of action items, as well as tasks in the Gantt chart, for overall project success.
Issues tracking	See the *Issue Tracking Process* in Appendix B for details on identifying and categorizing project issues. Basically, this is a way to track real-time issues. The objectives of having such a process include prioritizing activities, identifying cross-project influences, and maintaining visibility on key issues so that they are driven to resolution. Lessons learned in resolving issues can be added to the knowledge base to help with future similar situations and to keep different parts of the team from wasting time by revisiting closed issues.
Risk identification, assessment, and mitigation	See *Risk Management Workflow* (Chapter 8) for details. Risk management should be initiated during the tail end of the project planning process and reassessed periodically throughout the project. There are many benefits to employing a risk management process. They include setting realistic project expectations by maintaining visibility of risks, quicker recovery of problems through previously conceived contingency plans, and lower impact of potential problems through preventative actions. There are four basic parts to the Risk Management Workflow: 1. Identify potential risks. 2. Assess the risks. 3. Make plans to address the risks. 4. Reassess the risks throughout the project.
Project status reporting	See the *Project Status Reporting Process* in Appendix A for details. Status reporting is a key PM element during the execution phase of a project. The primary intent is to have a consistent mechanism for project managers to report their progress against plan. Using a consistent process en-

	ables status to be easily rolled up to the program and business levels.
Knowledge management	See *Lessons Learned Process* (Chapter 5) for details. Emerging and agile organizations that are developing new project management infrastructure will inevitably go through some iteration as the new PM processes are tuned to their project and business environment. The fast pace of the agile environment often encourages us to forget our mistakes and just move on. This approach is probably the most effective at solving the immediate problem at hand, but is generally detrimental to the long-term development and optimization of the infrastructure. While we may have the good intention of going back to amend the processes and practices after the dust settles, it is easy to forget or never find the time to do so. The process should therefore be designed to be "light" enough so that it can be easily and frequently used to capture the lessons learned from the most recent projects and other significant events.
Meeting minutes	See *Project Communications Plan* (Chapter 4) for details. Meeting minutes, when captured properly, provide an excellent condensed history of a project. While we don't usually plan to look back very often, when we must, good meeting minutes are incredibly valuable. Additionally, the process of taking, condensing, and distributing meeting minutes is good discipline for project managers and helps set team expectations and tone for meetings. All project meeting minutes should be archived and made accessible to the team.
Meeting calendar	See *Project Communications Plan* (Chapter 4) for details. In an agile environment where there are numerous interlinked projects progressing simultaneously, it is necessary to coordinate communications/meetings at the portfolio-level, as well as at the project-level. Without this higher-level meeting coordination, it is very possible that the organization will experience redundancy on some issues while letting others slip through the cracks. The program should maintain a rolling meeting calendar, viewable by all team members, showing all of the various meetings taking place, their objectives, facilitator, and primary attendees.

Reports

Overview	This section represents all of the reports (organized and actionable information) that can be generated from the PM

data previously collected after it's been properly analyzed and put into consistent templates by the Program Analyst.

The Program Analyst and Process Developer should work together to understand the needs of their customers and continually improve the reports to meet their requirements. A few core reports are described below, but many other custom reports can be created as well.

Portfolio view	See the *Portfolio Prioritization Process* in Appendix D for details. This core report is designed to provide a one-page snapshot of all program activity. It is broken down into several categories: **Strategy:** The high-level goals of the business and the approach for attaining them **Business Objectives:** Concrete deliverables and/or milestones that, once achieved, will lead to the attainment of the business strategy **Programs:** A grouping of projects that, taken together, will lead to fulfillment of one or more deliverables/milestones required of a business objective **Active Projects:** Those that are staffed and actively being managed. **Inactive Projects:** Those that have been identified to be critical to overall success, but for which there is no current staffing. These projects are kept on the portfolio view so that they do not lose visibility.
Program status update	This core report is basically a roll-up or summary of multiple project status reports to the program level. It is designed to give a high-level snapshot of the progress to plan across multiple projects simultaneously. It includes general (Red-Yellow-Green) status and a summary of current issues and risks, but leaves out the details included in the individual project status reports.
Resource allocations	This core report is designed to give a high-level view of resource utilization approximately 3 to 6 months out, based on current project plans. A bar chart or pie chart graphic is very effective at conveying this type of information. A primary objective of this report is to provide a basis for an operational hiring plan for the program.
Management dashboard	This report is a combination of the Portfolio View, Program Status, and Resource Allocation reports. Through analysis and consolidation of related information, the Program Analyst highlights the critical few program elements that need management attention.

11

AGILE PORTFOLIO MANAGEMENT: ALIGNING TACTICAL PROJECTS WITH BUSINESS STRATEGY

Up to now we've been discussing what to do within the project management realm to achieve agility. The focus has been on managing a single project. However, truly agile organizations do not execute projects only one at a time. They execute the right mix of projects to achieve their high-level business objectives. It doesn't help the organization much if you crank through complex projects, only to realize that there are still gaps in the overall business solution. This is the domain of portfolio management—creating, organizing, and prioritizing the portfolio of projects to best meet company objectives.

Portfolio Management

You will recall that our initial definition of an agile project revolved around internal and external uncertainty. Internal uncertainty is specific to the project itself, while external uncertainty is related to the environment in which the project operates. This external environment includes the cross-functional organization running the project, the corporate parent, competition, customers, and the overall economic environment. Portfolio management encompasses those areas that are external to the project but still within the sponsor organization, such as other (related) projects, business strategy, and organizational resources. Figure 11-1 depicts how a project might fit into a larger portfolio of projects within the parent company, as well as its various external influences. Note that external influences to the project are not always external to the parent company.

Many companies treat portfolio management as an independent process—often an exercise that takes place during the annual business-planning cycle. Taken in this context, I probably would not include portfolio management in this book. However, in the accelerated business environment, the project is the business—or, more appropriately, the projects are the business (see Chapter 3). This expanded view of agile PM will further facilitate the quest for organizational agility by ensuring that the company's scarce resources are best utilized not merely within a single project, but within the company's portfolio of projects. This concept takes on an even greater importance as changes in the business environment become increasingly rapid. An annual review of the portfolio is no longer adequate. You must be prepared

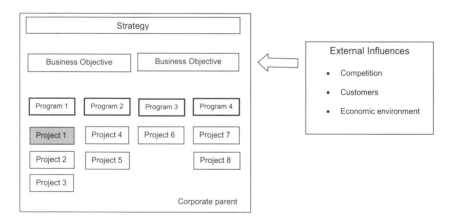

Figure 11-1. A general portfolio management structure showing the alignment of high-level strategy, business objectives, programs, and individual projects.

to reprioritize projects, as needed, whenever events cause selection criteria to change value, or criteria weighting to change, or new criteria to be introduced.

Portfolio management is a key linkage between business strategy and tactical project execution, and it is much more effective than trying to tie individual projects directly to business strategy. In the ideal case, strategy would be translated into business objectives, which would be translated into programs, then to projects. All of these would be filtered through the portfolio management machine for optimization. You would then execute your projects, and business strategy would be successfully achieved. However, as you know, the ideal world and the agile world are two different environments. Projects originate from all sorts of places. Business strategies change more frequently than we would like. Competition forces us to change plans on the fly. What worked last year may no longer be applicable today. Resources are available, and then they're not. Or they get reallocated, causing a ripple effect. All of these realities call for an agile portfolio management process.

Agile Strategy

Use portfolio management to create the vital linkage between business strategy and the tactical execution of individual projects.

In the classic project environment, the waterfall of information flows mostly downhill from high-level strategy to business objectives to the program to the individual project (see Figure 11-2). The real value of the portfolio management process is in keeping all of these areas aligned. In this case, most of the aligning happens at the bottom level, where the individual projects reside. Since the classic project operates in a generally more mature industry, it is less likely to be directly influenced by an event outside of the company. The high-level strategy, however, is very open to influence by external events. Therefore, changes in the classic portfolio are more likely to be initiated upstream than downstream.

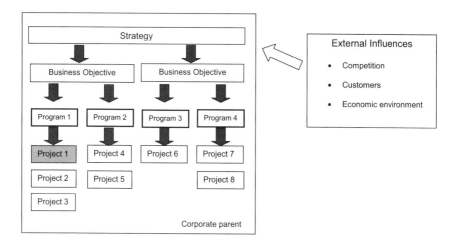

Figure 11-2. In classic portfolio management, external influences start at the top and flow downstream.

> **Externally influenced changes in the classic paradigm are more likely to be felt initially at the strategy level, then cascade down to the project level.**

On the other hand, agile projects, which are more attuned to external influences to start with, are more prone to feel their direct effect at the project level (see Figure 11-3). They also tend to be breaking new technological ground, giving them a potentially greater importance to the overall business schema. All of these dimensions have the power to cause a ripple effect upstream (see Figure 11-4). Essentially, an unexpected change in an individual project could create a business strategy change in the agile environment.

> **Externally influenced changes in the agile paradigm are felt at the project level, as well as at the strategy and objectives levels. This, in turn, can create an upstream ripple effect from the project level to the strategy level.**

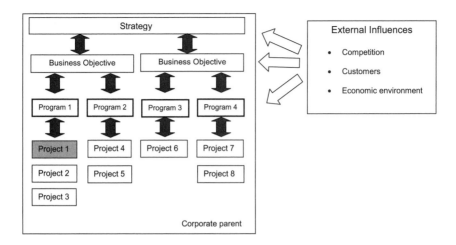

Figure 11-3. In agile portfolio management, external influences are felt directly at the top and bottom and subsequently flow both downstream and upstream.

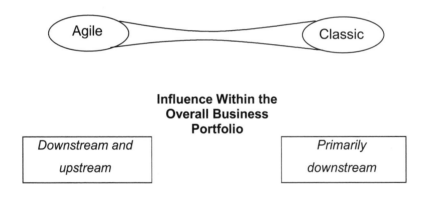

Figure 11-4. The direction of influence in an agile versus classic portfolio.

In industries where agility is truly required, portfolio management inevitably consumes an increasingly significant portion of the senior program manager's time. In slower-moving industries, however, port-folio management will most likely remain within executive manage-ment's domain. Program and project managers will provide data on the projects, business/financial analysts will weigh the criteria, execu-tive management will select/prioritize the projects, and then the pro-gram/project managers will execute the modified portfolio. It is not unusual for this process to take two to three months to come full circle. An annual portfolio review that takes three months may be tolerable (and appropriate) in some industries, but in a fast-paced business environment, this is a recipe for failure. (See Figure 11-5.) Because of the high rate of uncertainty and fierce competition, it will be necessary to do two things:

1. Integrate portfolio management into the day-to-day/month-to-month project management process.
2. Bring portfolio management, at least partially, under the umbrella of the program manager.

Agile Strategy

Integrate portfolio management into the routine project management process, via the operational infrastructure as much as possible, to avoid the "once annually" portfolio review.

A good project management infrastructure (see Chapter 10) provides a common framework for efficiently processing day-to-day project data, thus freeing up the valuable time of the project manager to keep a vigilant view on the project and the environment external to the project. The portfolio that surrounds a project is, in fact, one of those critical, external elements that must be watched by the project manager. By integrating portfolio management criteria into the proj-

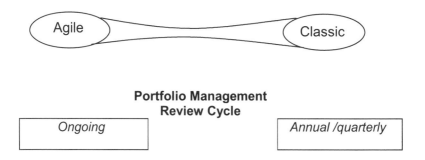

Figure 11-5. The portfolio review cycle in an agile versus classic portfolio.

ect management infrastructure, you let the infrastructure's systems and the program analyst process the routine data. In this way, the portfolio is constantly and efficiently monitored for changes in strategy, weighting criteria, or the projects themselves that may trigger the need for a reprioritization/rebalancing of the portfolio. Therefore, the project or program manager only needs to get actively involved when certain triggers are hit. For example, let's say a deal is closed that requires a new customer project to be initiated immediately. There are no resources available, so they must be pulled from an active project, effectively putting it on hold. This on-hold project, in turn, is a dependency for another internal project. The triggering event for this second project is the delay in the first project (its dependency) and would be flagged by the program analyst. At this point, the program manager would get involved to determine if it still made sense to push forward with the second project, or if the portfolio should be rebalanced until the first project is restaffed.

Agile Strategy

Make portfolio management part of the program manager's responsibilities. Since the program manager works in the middle between the high-level strategy and tactical projects, she is best able to manage the two-way interactions and impacts between them.

By bringing portfolio management under the wing of the program manager, you accomplish two things. First, you significantly reduce the end-to-end cycle time of reacting to a change. Second, you reinforce the concepts that the projects are the business and that program managers need to be aware of the business environment external to the actual projects. These concepts involve a major role change for most program managers (and functional managers) and should be approached with caution. In Chapter 5, when we discussed having the project manager take an outward orientation, it was primarily to monitor external factors so that he can make appropriate adjustments within his project. Now I am suggesting that program managers (who are generally more senior than project managers) be given responsibility for overseeing the company's project portfolio, which is really an overlap of functional and executive management's traditional roles (see Figure 11-6).

This shifting of responsibilities is necessary in order to increase overall organizational efficiency, and there are a few practical ways to implement it. The most direct implementation is to give the program manager responsibility for identifying triggers anywhere within the corporate/business environment that cause the portfolio to be revisited and for making recommendations to rebalance/reprioritize the project portfolio. Executive/functional management would still make the decision on whether (and how) to act on the recommendations. This scenario develops the program manager. It pulls her deeper into the business decision-making process and, simultaneously, frees up executive management from focusing on the tactical portfolio management process, so executives can instead spend more energy on matters such as understanding the customer's needs, the competition, resources, and the macro business environment.

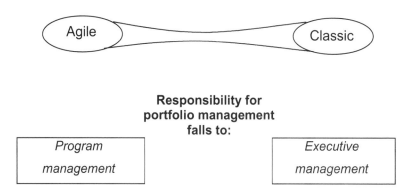

Figure 11-6. Portfolio management responsibility in an agile versus classic portfolio.

Agile Strategy

Ease into agile portfolio management by delegating responsibility to program management for identifying triggers, performing analysis, and making recommendations, while maintaining ultimate decision making at the executive level.

Another possibility is to give ongoing tactical portfolio management responsibility to the functional/executive manager who is closest to the core program objectives and/or who owns the majority of resources involved. This shift is taking place more and more frequently because these managers already have a good understanding of the business thresholds, especially resource-related ones, that trigger portfolio rebalancing. By providing them with real-time information via the project management infrastructure (which is now integrated with portfolio management), they will be able to effectively monitor and adjust the portfolio on a fairly continuous basis to meet business objectives.

These are just a few ideas for getting started with integrating project management and portfolio management. Every organization is somewhat unique, and the actual implementation must be tailored to that business. However, the bottom-line message is that integrating portfolio management with project management is an efficient way to ensure that your valuable resources are working on the right projects.

Agile Strategy

Another approach to implementing portfolio management is to delegate this responsibility to the functional manager closest to the overall project set. This not only gets functional management more deeply involved at the strategy and project levels, but also paves the way for establishing a project-based organization.

Creating Your Portfolio View

When getting started with portfolio management, or when performing a comprehensive review of a current process, it makes sense to start at or near the top. However, this isn't always necessary, especially if you're just getting started with formal portfolio management. In this case, it may make sense to start from both ends, and see if and where they meet. The general hierarchy for mapping a project portfolio is strategy, then business objectives, then programs, and finally projects (see Figure 11-7). In the final portfolio, you should have a clear understanding of how every project you're working on supports one or more strategies. For this reason, the result of this mapping process is referred to as the Portfolio View.

One approach is to list your business strategies across the top of a whiteboard. Then lay out the high-level business objectives under each strategy. Under each business objective, list programs and then projects. This sounds pretty easy, but it may become confusing. You may discover that things don't line up into neat columns. Some projects map to multiple programs; some programs map to multiple objectives; and some things don't map to anything. Very soon, you may have a complex and tangled web that will make your head spin.

Because the agile portfolio is influenced just as much from the bottom levels of the organization (where projects reside) as the top, you may find that the classic top-down methods of portfolio construction do not always work smoothly. You may find, for instance, that lower-level projects are significantly disjointed. There may be numerous, loosely linked efforts proceeding simultaneously without a strong objective tying them together. In this case, you would need to start at the bottom and first organize your projects, then your programs. You will probably identify some overlap as well as gaps that need to be

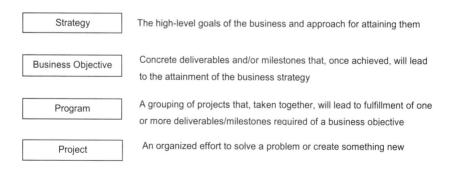

Figure 11-7. Portfolio mapping hierarchy.

addressed. At the same time, you may start to go down your list of business strategies and see if they meet the bottom-up projects and programs. Most likely, you won't have a clean linkup. You will have to work to get everything into alignment by nudging the project portfolio, the business strategy, or both.

The agile environment is one of discovery and breaking new ground. Its inherent nature encourages grass-roots efforts to address challenges. As project, program, portfolio, and executive managers, we need to recognize that not all projects will be driven from the top down. In fact, significant projects will initiate themselves among the core rank and file. Some of these grass-roots efforts may actually create a profound influence on top-level business strategies. In this situation, it is imperative that you initially construct your project portfolio with a strong bottom-up perspective (see Figure 11-8).

There are many ways to help organize your current portfolio, and all of them involve a little brute force and cranking through details. The exercise itself will involve many parts of the organization, and it can be very beneficial, if conducted correctly and tactfully. Organizing your portfolio "correctly" means that all linkages and dependencies are captured and understood. It is especially important to recognize the lower-level, interproject dependencies that are often overlooked but, if not understood, can end up wreaking havoc on a higher-level program or objective. Working "tactfully" means that portfolio management is an emotional and political exercise. You need to take an objective perspective when creating your overall portfolio mapping.

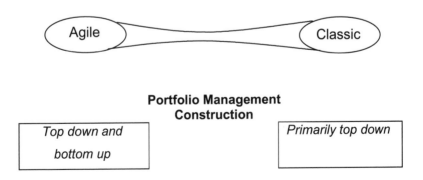

Figure 11-8. Portfolio construction in an agile versus classic environment.

If you are too subjective or let personal preferences, pet projects, or a silo mentality enter into the mix, then you may find that every project supports every strategy and that all are equally important. This may be true, but probably isn't, which means that you won't get the added value that you need from portfolio management.

In-depth discussions to prioritize projects are required to get and keep the portfolio aligned. These efforts may be painful and unpopular, but they are essential to maintain business agility.

Making sense out of a tangled web of projects is hard work, but you need to do it. You'll learn a lot about what your organization is working on, what it thinks is important, and how it works. You will probably even revisit some of your high-level strategies. This is all good. Additionally, once you've worked through this process, you will have created your Portfolio View, which provides an excellent, one-page, big-picture view of your business (for a more detailed example of a Portfolio View, see Appendix D). This, in turn, enables your portfolio management process to be integrated into your day-to-day operational project management processes for maintenance and reporting purposes.

Maintaining Alignment Through Review and Prioritization

Completing the initial creation of your business project portfolio is a solid milestone; however, maintaining the portfolio will require considerable effort. There are two basic mechanisms for keeping the elements of your portfolio in alignment as the various projects and the business move forward:

1. Ongoing project reviews

2. Periodic portfolio prioritization

Project reviews involve the ongoing monitoring of project status, milestones, and issues. When you are managing several agile projects simultaneously, you may find yourself addressing major project decision points almost constantly. As these significant events take place, you should not only be assessing their impact on the individual project, but also on the overall portfolio that is external to the project in question. If impacts on other projects are identified, then the project managers for those projects should be notified and apprised of the situation. The solution will likely involve some kind of joint effort or give-and-take between the two project teams. No matter what form the remediation takes, the key point is that the impact is identified and communicated in a timely manner. In this way, any ripple effect caused by a single project will quickly propagate through the portfolio and then settle out, hopefully before the next impact event.

Agile Strategy

When conducting individual project reviews or status reporting, include a portfolio element to ensure that the project manager assesses how her project may affect others, and how they might affect hers.

Portfolio prioritization usually takes the form of a periodic review meeting chaired by a program manager and attended by the executive and/or functional management team. The goal of these review meetings is to reassess the priorities of the business objectives, programs, and projects, based on any changes driven by internal or external events since the last prioritization. This is a top-down process that gives a quick overview of the various elements of the portfolio, based on a few predetermined evaluation criteria. So, while this is largely a qualitative process, there is a quantitative dimension to it that helps keep emotions and pet projects in check. The evaluation criteria should be selected to reflect the business goals, as well as the realities of project management, most notably resources and progress to plan. An example of a workflow and template for a project prioritization process in provided in Appendix D.

The results of the reprioritization may have their own impacts and ripple effects on the project portfolio. Likely project adjustments coming out of a reprioritization include schedule and resource shifts, as well as project cancellation or postponement.

Agile Strategy

Conduct periodic portfolio prioritizations based on the top-down approach of systematically looking at high-level business goals and organizational resources, to ensure that the organization continues to efficiently advance its highest-priority projects.

In an agile environment, you cannot afford the inefficiencies of working on things that do not contribute to the business objectives. By employing the bottom-up, project review–driven approach to portfolio adjustments, combined with the top-down prioritization process, you will have a much better chance of keeping your high-level objectives aligned with your tactical projects.

Resources—The Preeminent Agile Criteria

There are many different criteria used in the construction and prioritization of a project portfolio. Some notable ones include resources, strategic fit, competition, pipeline value, return on investment (ROI), and risk. Of all of these criteria, resources have a unique impact in the agile environment. There are two reasons. First, agile portfolios tend to be made up of many small projects, as opposed to fewer larger projects in the classic paradigm. Second, the high uncertainty in the agile environment may cause projects to change, be canceled, expand, or be newly initiated. These changes happen on a continual basis. Both of these dynamics intersect with the allocation of resources.

Agile portfolios tend to be made up of many small yet related projects.

Since resources are limited, the rapid change of projects in the agile portfolio requires that resources be efficiently shifted between projects, as needed, to advance the overall portfolio (see Figure 11-9). To effectively manage resources across the agile portfolio, you must know where resources are currently allocated and anticipate where they may be needed in the future.

When trying to anticipate how resources may need to be reallocated, you should consider another distinction between the agile and classic environments. In the agile environment, project timelines are often pulled in, giving little time for the team to adjust; whereas in the classic environment, timeline shifts are almost always pushed out, giving the team time to react to the change. A typical driver for a rapid portfolio shift is the signing of a new sales deal. The instant energy generated by a potentially lucrative deal propagates a "drop everything and start working on this new project" reaction. This approach is only partially correct. You probably do want to start working on this new project as soon as possible, but you don't want to just drop everything. You want to cancel or postpone and, subsequently, shift resources from other projects where it makes sense and where there is the least impact on the overall business objectives.

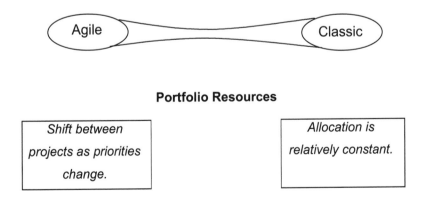

Figure 11-9. Portfolio resource allocation in an agile versus classic environment.

You are much more likely to see unexpected timeline shifts to the left in an agile environment versus a classic one.

In essence, you want to be creating a portfolio plan that shows where your resources are being allocated at a macro level over the course of some time period. Once you have this information, you can determine funding needs and project plans based on various "what if" scenarios. I prefer to have a visual representation of this resource allocation. A portfolio-level Gantt chart, depicting each individual project as a single-line item, is a good way to gain a high-level view of your resource plan. It gives you a rough idea of project-to-resource density over time. The resource allocation to individual projects can be depicted as a color spectrum (e.g., light equals fewer resources, dark equals more resources) for a ballpark feel (see Figure 11-10), or exact percentages can be annotated in for more detail (see Figure 11-11).

Agile Strategy

Create a portfolio-level Gantt chart to get a high-level view of your resource allocations across the entire organization.

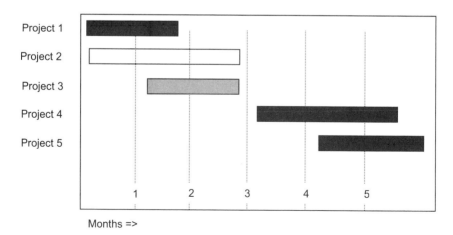

Months =>

Figure 11-10. Portfolio-level Gantt chart showing roughly estimated project/resource density over time.

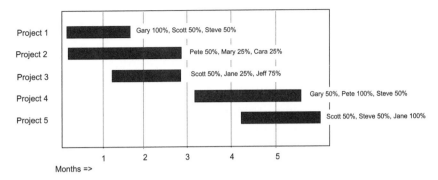

Figure 11-11. Portfolio-level Gantt chart showing rough resource usage over time.

By making the assumption that work level is constant, on average, for each resource for the duration of the project in question (which is an acceptable top-down estimation technique for agile environments), then you can create the portfolio-level Gantt chart, modified with the addition of resources to get a more detailed pictorial view of resource usage across the portfolio. Figure 11-11 is an example of the annotated format.

Let's examine how you might approach this task. Resource allocation is traditionally a detailed, bottom-up exercise starting at the task level and rolling up to the project and program levels. However, in agile PM, a top-down resource estimation is more appropriate. Spending inordinate time creating minute detail may be a wasted effort, if some external event creates a sudden change in the project plan.

The benefit of top-down estimation is that it is fast and doesn't require grinding out the task-level details. The downside is that it just isn't as accurate as bottom-up estimation. To compensate for this deficiency, we will look at a top-down estimate separately from both the project and portfolio perspectives, then compare results. If there are large discrepancies, we can revisit the estimate and make the necessary adjustments. If they are in agreement, then we have effectively increased our confidence level in the estimate by coming at it from two different angles.

Agile Strategy

Increase the confidence level of your top-down resource estimates by examining them from both the project level and portfolio level, then comparing results.

Project-Level Resource Estimation

You will recall that in our previous discussion of the Project Data Sheet (see Chapter 7), we used a top-down, project-level, resource estimation technique (see Figure 11-12). By aggregating all of the Project Data Sheets, the portfolio manager can get a roll-up estimate of resources at the portfolio level for a specific time period.

Portfolio-Level Resource Estimation

The primary difference in approaching resources from the portfolio level is in how and when you obtain the estimates. The project-level resource estimates were captured in the Project Data Sheet at the initiation of the project, and they may (or may not) have been updated since. If there are many projects, it could be a nuisance to regularly update resource estimates on multiple Project Data Sheets. You only want to have to go back to the PDS if you have reason to suspect that

Resources:
Provide an estimate of the resources (people and money) required to complete this project. People should be estimated using FTE (full time equivalent) months.

Resource:	S	O	N	D	J	F	M	A	M	J	J	A	Total
Project manager													
Team member #1													
Team member #2													
Team member #3													
Total FTE months													
Money ($)													

Figure 11-12. Top-down, project-level, resource estimation table from Project Data Sheet template.

the original estimate is out of date. It is much more palatable to regularly review resources at the portfolio-level. Figure 11-13 is an example of a format that can be used with team members to capture top-down resource estimates at the portfolio-level. This data can be displayed as a pie chart or bar graph, but its primary value is for comparison against the resource data from the project-level PDS roll-up in order to identify the need for revisiting a particular area.

Agile Strategy

Monitor your monthly (periodic) resource estimates at the portfolio level, and only revisit resources at the project level when a gross mismatch is identified between the two.

Resource Estimates and Multiple Pathways

Since the future pathways of individual projects, as well as the overall portfolio, are not fully predictable, it is often valuable to do a resource

Resources:
Provide an estimate of the time to be spent on the various projects for the next period. Resources should be estimated using FTE months.

Period: Month

Resource:	Project 1	Project 2	Project 3	Project 4	Project 5	Project 6	Project 7	Project 8	Project n	Total
Team member #1										
Team member #2										
Team member #3										
Team member #4										
Team member *n*										
Total FTE months										

Figure 11-13. Top-down, portfolio-level, resource estimation table for a specific period.

analysis based on various potential scenarios. (For example, the test phase of project 1 will only take one pass, the sales group will close the deal for project 2 next month, etc.). I've found that the most valuable analysis is to create a resource-by-resource (or role-by-role) trend over time in the form of a bar chart (see Figure 11-14). This will let you quickly see the loading of any specific resource, should a particular scenario come to fruition.

Other Typical Criteria

The specific weighting criteria used to manage a corporate project portfolio are dependent on the actual business/company and, generally, determined by executive management. A few of the more common criteria are strategic fit, ROI, and risk (among others), and they are largely addressed similarly in the agile or classic environment. As your portfolio management process matures, these criteria will become more detailed and business specific. The key points to consider are these: First, evaluating a project is different from evaluating a port-

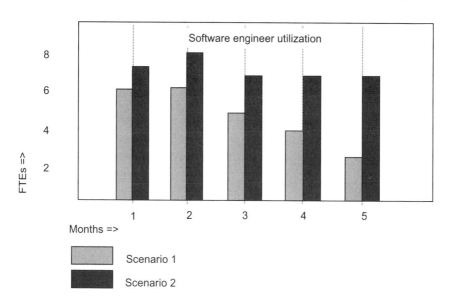

Figure 11-14. Portfolio-level Gantt chart showing rough resource usage over time.

folio. For instance, you may not be able to justify an individual project alone, but it is more than justified when viewed as part of a portfolio of projects with a common, higher-level objective. Second, the nature of the agile environment (high uncertainty with multiple pathways) makes the strategies and objectives more likely to require multiple, small projects rather than a single, large one (see Figure 11-15). This, in turn, makes agile projects more conducive to the use of a portfolio management approach instead of treating each individual project separately when evaluating the project's value to the business.

Successfully managing individual projects is only the start of a truly agile project-driven organization. Creating an agile portfolio management process will help ensure that the business is working on the right projects to attain its high-level objectives and business strategy. Integrating your portfolio management process with your project management processes will, in turn, provide the necessary, real-time linkages between the strategy and project levels of the business to keep them in alignment as business and project conditions change.

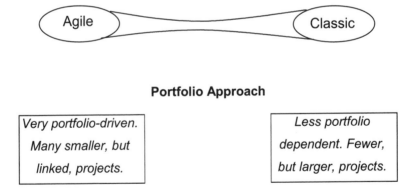

Figure 11-15. Approach to achieving high-level objectives through tactical projects in an agile versus classic environment.

Summary

❑ Portfolio management is a vital linkage between business strategy and tactical project execution.

❑ External influences in the agile paradigm are felt at the project level, as well as at the strategy and business objectives levels. This, in turn, can create an upstream ripple effect from the project level to the strategy level.

❑ In the agile environment, integrating the project management and portfolio management processes will lead to greater success in achieving business objectives and strategy.

❑ In the agile paradigm, objectives are often achieved through a portfolio of many smaller, but closely linked, projects.

❑ In the agile environment, portfolio management is an ongoing effort, often best managed by a portfolio program manager rather than executive management.

❑ It is critical to understand resource allocation in the agile environment so that resources can be efficiently shifted between projects, as necessary.

❑ Coming at the resource estimates from both the project and portfolio levels will increase your confidence in the results, as well as make the maintenance less painful for your team.

12

INTEGRATING PORTFOLIO AND PROJECT MANAGEMENT WITH THE PRODUCT DEVELOPMENT PROCESS FOR BUSINESS SUCCESS

In many technology companies, especially smaller ones, the project portfolio (and the business) revolves around R&D. This actually makes perfect sense, since it is the technology that provides the competitive advantage for the company. The problem is in balancing the desire for innovation against the need for process (see Figure 12-1). Most creative engineers and scientists would much prefer to focus on the next technological breakthrough than portfolio management, project management, or any other process for that matter. These processes are often considered a necessary evil, and they are given less attention than is usually required to make them successful. Our quandary, then, is this: Do we emphasize the importance of project and portfolio management at the risk of killing innovation, or do we take a hands-off approach and encourage pure innovation, with the hopes that what is developed will, indeed, support the business strat-

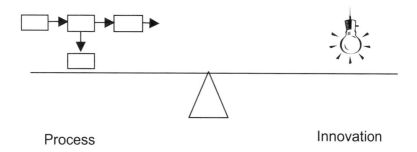

Process   Innovation

Figure 12-1. Balancing process and innovation.

egy? These are tough questions that permeate many technology businesses. Of course, the answers are probably somewhere in between.

Integrating Process and Innovation

Balancing the needs of the process against the needs of innovation is on the minds of technical project managers everywhere. The problem with this approach is that it implies that process (in this case, the portfolio management process, but it could also be the project management process) and innovation are two separate entities with different requirements that need to be balanced. This, in turn, suggests that process and innovation have separate owners and are at odds with each other—which is definitely not a recipe for agility. Much of the agile paradigm is about integrating activities, processes, and roles so that the right information flows in a timely fashion to whomever needs it. In this case, we should be looking for ways to integrate process and innovation in a supportive manner instead of trying to balance them against one another.

From the project team perspective, project management can be justified as a tool that helps the team meet the immediate project milestones. Portfolio management, on the other hand, is one step further removed from the team. It is more related to business-level objectives than project-level ones. This means that portfolio management activities are generally a lower priority than project management activities to the team, making it that much more difficult to instill an effective process.

Most companies that are successful in integrating process and innovation have managers and project managers with the right mix of technical, business, and interpersonal skills. These gifted individuals have earned credibility within their organizations by demonstrating subject matter and management expertise. They consistently add value and a host of other leadership qualities to the organization. The problem with depending on individuals to integrate innovation and process is that it is difficult to help people progress up the skill ladder. Experience is one common denominator of successful project managers in R&D, and even experience doesn't guarantee that they will be successful. Training certainly can help, but there isn't much training available on this specific topic of how to meld technical/subject matter capabilities and business/management processes, since it's tightly related to company-specific process development. We need to find new ways to help project managers become more effective at integrating the creative and business needs without relying solely on interpersonal skills.

While *process* is somewhat of an outlawed word in R&D, most good R&D managers realize that some level of process is necessary to efficiently develop good products. In many industries, a well-designed product development process (PDP) is mandated by government regulations, or it may be required to obtain certain certifications, such as ISO 9001. In the end, it just makes good business sense to have a robust product development process, since the structured methodology will help ensure that your product meets customer needs, functions as advertised, and is supportable and manufacturable. Most R&D organizations already have some type of product development process in place and in use. If there is any process that will be tolerated or even embraced in R&D, it is the product development process. Rather than inflicting the additional layers of portfolio management or project management process on the poor engineers, you should be looking for ways to extend their product development process to cover key elements of these other processes (see Figure 12-2.) In this way, the importance and requirements for effective portfolio and proj-

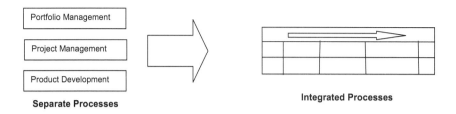

Figure 12-2. Integrating project management and portfolio management into the product development process.

ect management are more easily digested, thus creating a more optimized and integrated process.

Acknowledgment of the product development process as the core business/technical process for the company (and also building on it) is often the most effective business solution for technology-centric companies. By cleanly extending the product development process to encompass key dimensions of portfolio management and project management, you add value to the established core R&D process (PDP), advance the effectiveness of R&D managers and project managers, and create the foundation for effective portfolio and project decision making.

Agile Strategy

Integrate core elements of project management and portfolio management into the already-established product development process, rather than attempt to establish two new processes.

Integrating Portfolio Management Into the Product Development Process

There are probably numerous ways to extend the product development process to encompass portfolio management, but one critical goal that we are trying to achieve is ongoing portfolio management versus the annual portfolio review approach. Generally, this means monitoring and analyzing the situation and events on a regular basis.

One relatively easy way to start toward an integrated solution is to look for ways to tie portfolio management decisions to major project reviews. Most product development processes in the technology space are based on the stage-gate concept, which requires formal reviews at predesignated milestone points before the project team can continue to the next stage (see Figure 12-3). This is a logical point to extend the normal stage-gate criteria to include a review of how the project fits into the portfolio, how recent project decisions may affect other parts of the portfolio, and how other portfolio decisions may affect this project. In theory, this is not quite as continuous a process as you may want, since portfolio reviews only come at stage-gates and then only for the projects in question. However, depending on the number of projects running simultaneously in your portfolio, progressions to stage-gates may happen as often as monthly, which is certainly much better than only addressing the portfolio once a year.

Agile Strategy

Tie portfolio reviews to stage-gates as a first step toward integrating portfolio management into the product development process.

Stage-gate review meetings should be scheduled at regular periodic intervals (i.e., on the first Thursday of each month), so key managers can get them on their calendars; however, only projects that are at a stage-gate need to be discussed. In fact, at any particular stage-gate

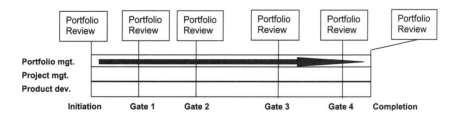

Figure 12-3. Portfolio reviews tied to stage-gates.

review meeting, only one or a few projects may be specifically reviewed, though you can focus part of that review on how the specific project affects and is affected by the rest of the business project portfolio. Even when a minority of the total projects is reviewed, the discussion on interactions with the rest of the portfolio may extend to the majority, if not all, of the portfolio projects.

The first few times that you use this integrated process, you may find that most of the discussion is off-the-cuff or consists of brainstorming. Once project teams realize how interdependent they are and how much they can learn from each other, you can better facilitate a learning process. Project teams will become better able to communicate specific dependencies on other projects or areas of interest to the other project teams in the portfolio, as well as to the stage-gate review committee. By reviewing any particular project's status against a "master dependency" list from the larger project portfolio, project managers can quickly identify issues and synergies that may not otherwise have been specifically identified or discussed.

The idea here is for the project team and stage-gate committee to identify issues (based on the master dependency list), follow them up with a discussion to qualify the discovery, and then scheduling time offline from the stage-gate meeting for further investigation with the appropriate parties. This process tends to help individual projects come together as a single portfolio with common objectives. The result not only adds value to the project, it is partially a criterion for progressing to the next phase.

For example, let's say that the project under review is one of five projects that together comprise a program to develop an ultra-light notebook computer. The team responsible for the video display subsystem comes to the stage-gate review meeting having met all of its objectives for the previous stage. Additionally, it has created a project plan (i.e., a Project Data Sheet) for the next stage and is ready to begin executing on it upon receiving approval from the stage-gate committee, which it fully expects to receive. The video display design is right on target for all specifications except one, steady-state power, which is on the high end of the tolerance but still within spec. The video team considers this a low priority since it is still within spec.

This issue, however, comes up at the stage-gate review meeting during a review of the "potential impacts to other portfolio projects." The technical leader from the power-supply team realizes that this could be a critical issue because his team has been considering lowering the steady-state power specification to a point that would put the video display out of spec. A discussion ensues and it is determined that the video team, while meeting its own objectives, should not continue further development until the steady-state power question is resolved.

This example demonstrates how being cognizant of the potential impacts your project may have on other projects in the portfolio, and actively communicating those impacts to others, can help optimize the overall portfolio. This situation may have had a different outcome had the power-supply team identified steady-state power as a potential problem on the master dependency list, with a comment such as "Review all steady-state power requirements with power-supply team before finalizing designs." In this way, the issue could be identified prior to the stage-gate review meeting. Subsequently, it may have been resolved before the meeting as well.

Agile Strategy

Develop and maintain a "master dependency" list for the portfolio, then have project teams address how their projects affect and are affected by this list at each stage-gate.

Integrating Project Management Into the Product Development Process

It is in the tactical planning and management of individual projects where any new ideas or issues that were identified at the stage-gate/portfolio review are acted on. To this end, coming out of the stage-gate is generally a good point at which to make detailed modifications to your project plan (see Figure 12-4).

To effectively get the outputs from a stage-gate/portfolio review input into the detailed planning for the next project stage, you must

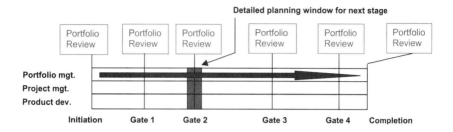

Figure 12-4. Phase-to-phase detailed project planning.

clearly articulate how the project management process will be integrated with the product development process. If you don't, valuable information can slip through the cracks and won't be addressed. One method I have found effective is to use the Project Data Sheet (PDS) format to create a new subproject for each new stage. This means that you will have one Project Data Sheet and high-level plan for the whole project, plus a sub-PDS and detailed plan for each stage. The executive summary format of the PDS makes it ideally suited for presentation and discussion with the stage-gate committee, as well as providing an organized framework for making modifications based on the aforementioned discussion.

Agile Strategy

Use Project Data Sheets to define each project stage as a subproject, to ensure that outputs from a stage-gate/portfolio review are integrated into the detailed planning for the next stage.

The extension of the stage-gate product development process described in this chapter will help you better manage your projects and portfolio on an ongoing basis, while maintaining a focus on the critical technical and innovative engines of your company. In today's competitive and uncertain business environment, innovation alone will not win the day. Product development needs to reach outside of R&D, create a linkage, and become immersed in the business environment. Gifted managers (product *and* project managers) often create this necessary linkage, but they will eventually be stretched too thin. Extending your product development process by integrating portfolio management and project management is one way to support these leaders, as well as broaden the bridge so that other project managers and team leads can help maintain this critical connection.

Summary

- ❑ Extending your product development process by integrating portfolio and project management is a light and effective way to introduce these concepts to the highly technical-driven organization.
- ❑ Many organizations maintain this integration by relying on project and product managers with the right combination of technical, business, and interpersonal skills, but employing this approach alone is not easily scalable.
- ❑ Stage-gate review meetings are a good place to integrate portfolio reviews into the product development process.
- ❑ Planning each project stage as a distinct subproject ensures that outputs from the stage-gate/portfolio review get integrated into the detailed plans for the next stage.

CONCLUSION

The most innovative companies of today and tomorrow will continue to push the project management envelope. For them, being able to effectively define, plan, and execute projects in a dynamic and fast-paced environment will be the difference between merely surviving and flourishing. The individuals leading these groundbreaking efforts know that their projects are challenging the status quo and that the classic PM thinking "just doesn't feel right." Project management is no longer just an academic exercise; it is needs to be a tactical tool that will help organizations reach their goals. Only those approaches that resonate with the team and organization will be given serious consideration, with techniques that create synergy between *process* and *creative freedom* being paramount. Agile PM swings the pendulum back to the creative side, while remaining in the background to facilitate project and organizational success.

While the theory of project management discusses the full project lifecycle, the practical application has largely focused on the *planning* stage. This focus is reflected and propagated by the predominant project management tools on the market, which are principally designed to automate planning activities such as timeline creation and resource allocation. However, in agile project environments, successful project management requires a shift of focus to the *execution* stage, because the inherent uncertainty of the environment places limits on how far into the future you can effectively plan your project. Agility is about making the right decisions during project execution (as well as planning); agile PM is about creating the environment and tools to support those decisions.

The successful companies of the future will move to better integrate their business and project decision making, thus creating real-time and two-way feedback between the project and the business. To this end, they will have to redefine traditional roles, organize around projects differently, and develop a new infrastructure that rethinks project definition and planning efforts in such a way as to support the execution efforts.

Taking the first step on the way to agility will be easy. Most likely, it will be energizing. Innovative organizations always appreciate new ideas, including ways to reap greater rewards from their investments in project management. They are also looking for the leaders who will champion these new ideas for the business. Agile project management is an evolution that is already under way in the subconscious of many project managers and organizations. This book documents some of the practices, tools, and attitudes that I've seen used successfully in agile environments. It is my hope that you will take some of these ideas, customize them to your unique business, and improve your overall project management effectiveness.

APPENDIX A

PROJECT STATUS REPORTING PROCESS

Status reporting is a key project management element during the execution phase of a project. The primary intent of a status reporting process is to have a consistent mechanism for project managers to report the project's progress to plan. Using a consistent process enables status to be easily rolled up to the program and business levels.

This process is used in conjunction with the included status report template. An electronic copy of this process and template can be downloaded from www.xocp.com.

Status Reporting Overview

Objectives   To communicate to the team and management:

1. How the project is doing against plan
2. What issues are currently being dealt with
3. What risks have been identified and what is being done about them
4. What changes have made to the plan since the last status report
5. What impact recent events related to this project may have on other projects in the portfolio

Prerequisites	Before initiating this process, ensure that you have a plan. This means, at a minimum, that you have a Project Data Sheet (PDS) completed for your project and a detailed Gantt chart, if necessary.
Resolution of common confusion	This process is sometimes referred to as a *progress reporting* process and sometimes as a *status reporting* process. For our purposes, these terms are synonymous and refer to your progress (or status) against your predetermined plan. Are you on track to meet your next milestone date? Are you ahead of schedule? Are you behind schedule? And why?
	The term *status* is often confused with *accomplishments*. Accomplishments are commonly reported to management, and they usually consist of a list of items that you have accomplished or finished since your last report. This list of accomplishments may or may not be relevant to your project status. This report should not discuss accomplishments that are not part of the project plan or that are not related to a project action item, issue, or risk.
Why accomplishment reporting is still needed	Now that we have emphasized that the intent of status reporting is to communicate *status to plan* and not *accomplishments,* it is important to note that acknowledgment of accomplishments is still necessary and even desired. Here are a few reasons why reporting on accomplishments is needed:

1. Functional managers usually want to know what their people have been doing and what they have accomplished.
2. People feel good when they have accomplished something, and being able to communicate that to a forum of their peers is a form of recognition.
3. To be able to fully evaluate a team member's performance and contribution, you must know what they have accomplished, as well as how well they have delivered to plan.

Non-project related accomplishments should be reported to functional management rather than project management, which is why you should use a different mechanism. While there may be some overlap, separating general accomplishments from project status reporting will help clarify and focus both reports, thus facilitating better team/management discussions.

Completing the Status Reporting Template

Project name	Enter the project name as it appears on the Project Data Sheet (PDS).
Date	Enter the date the progress report was completed.
Status summary	Assign a general status to the project for the current date. For example: **Green:** The project is on schedule (with all milestones-to-date) and is on track to meet the next milestone date. **Yellow:** The project is behind schedule, but the team feels that it's possible to get back on schedule in the near future. **Red:** The project is behind schedule and the team does not think it will be able to get back on schedule without some major help or an extension of the timeline.
Status comments	Describe your progress against your plan. Are you on schedule, ahead of schedule, or behind schedule? If you are behind schedule, why? And what are you doing about it? If your intention is to revise your plan, then that should also be discussed here.
Priority	This is the status assigned to your project during the *Portfolio Prioritization Process* in Appendix D. Although that process uses a numerical scoring method, the project management team should translate that data into a High-Medium-Low rating for the status report so that the priority is easily grasped by a reader not familiar with the details of the prioritization process. If you are not using the portfolio prioritization process, you should still assign a priority based on the project's value to the organization, as compared to other projects.
Projected completion date	Enter the date that your current timeline shows you completing your project.
Original estimated completion date	Enter the date that you originally planned on completing your project.
Milestones	The milestones can be pulled directly from the Project Data Sheet. They can be represented graphically or in bullet-list fashion. Include target completion dates for each milestone and whether they have been completed. The goal here is an easily readable (i.e., graphical) snapshot of the project's progress against plan at the milestone level.

Issues	Describe the *current* issues you are encountering and how you are addressing them. If you need help or need the issue escalated, then that should also be mentioned here. Issues can be pulled directly from the issues matrix. See the *Issue Tracking Process* in Appendix B for details.
Risks	Describe potential future events that could have a negative (or positive) affect on your project. Also describe the *impact* to the project if the event were to occur and the *probability* that the event will occur. Describe any mitigation efforts that you are taking to minimize the chance of the risk event occurring. Describe your contingency plan should the risk event occur. Risks, mitigations, and contingencies can be pulled directly from the risk matrix. See the *Risk Management Workflow* (Chapter 8) for details.
External impact	Describe any potential impact that this project may have on other projects in the portfolio, or on the business in general, due to recent developments described previously. As much as possible, try to identify the specific projects, project managers, technical leaders, or functional managers affected so that appropriate notification can take place.

(Project Name) Status Report (date)

Status: *Yellow*

Projected completion date: **July 14, 2003**

Priority: *High*

Original estimated completion: **July 8, 2003**

Status comments:

Describe progress against the plan (i.e., on track, ahead of schedule, or behind schedule). Any variance to the plan should be explained briefly here.

Milestones:

Insert milestones graphs.

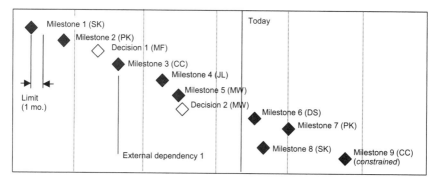

Issues:

List open issues here. Pull this information from the Issues Tracking report (fields: Issue, Owner, and Notes).

Risks:

List risks here. Pull this information from the Risks Management report.

External impact:

Describe any potential impact that this project may have on other projects in the portfolio, or on the business in general, due to recent developments.

APPENDIX B

ISSUE TRACKING PROCESS

Systematically identifying and tracking project issues facilitates the efficient resolution of critical problems and is therefore necessary for good project management. In fact, many people say that driving issue resolution is one of the most important responsibilities of the project manager. This process discusses a basic method for efficiently tracking issues, as well as clarifying the confusion that often exists in distinguishing an *issue*, *task*, or *risk*. An electronic copy of this process and template can be downloaded from www.xocp.com.

Definitions

Overview	When you mention the term *issue* to a group of people, each person may be imagining something different, and in a certain context, each of them is probably correct. Therefore, it is critical to proper communication that everyone uses the same definition. This process uses the following definitions.
Issue: Category 1	A technical or business situation with *no known solution* that is negatively affecting a project.
Issue: Category 2	A technical or business situation that is negatively affecting a project for which there is a *proposed solution* that hasn't been fully implemented yet.

Issue: Category 3	A technical or business situation that is *out of your control* and negatively affecting a project.

Common Confusions

Tasks versus issues	Confusing *tasks* and *issues* is a common mistake. Tasks have these common characteristics:

❑ They can be and should be planned (whereas issues are unplanned).

❑ You mostly know how to complete tasks (issues may have unknown solutions).

❑ They are in your control to complete (issues may be out of your control).

For example, an overdue task is not an issue per se, but rather a symptom of an issue. The real issue might be that resources were diverted from your project to a higher-priority one (something out of your control), or you encountered an unexpected obstacle for which there is no obvious way to circumvent (an unknown solution). Project managers should be on the lookout for symptoms, but they need to dig down and identify the root issue.

Risks versus issues	Risks are forward looking, whereas issues are real-time. A risk may, and often does, turn into an issue; however, project managers should strive to not let this happen. By definition, a risk is an unplanned future event that either positively or negatively affects your project. While the risk event is not officially planned (as part of your WBS and Gantt chart), it has been identified (how else would you know about it?). Once a risk is identified, project managers should create contingency plans for the risk. Then, if and when the risk event does happen, it does not turn into an issue but rather triggers the contingency plan, which should neutralize the unplanned risk event. See the *Risk Management Workflow* in Chapter 8 for further details on risks.

Why We Track Issues

Issues need visibility until they are resolved	One of the most valuable contributions that a project manager can make is simply to keep all key project indicators visible. Once projects leave the planning phase and enter the execution phase, things can start to get very

chaotic. Priorities can change rapidly and issues that are receiving appropriate attention one minute are shuffled below others the next. This does not necessarily mean that an issue is no longer important, just that it's become old news. The project manager must give attention and visibility to even aging issues until they are fully resolved.

Issues are often interrelated	Issues tend to lead to more issues. As complications increase, it is important that the project manager be able to rise above the dust and understand how the many issues and plans are interrelated. If issues are simply handed out to various individuals to handle, they may never see how what they are working on affects what someone else is working on until it is too late.
Issues are a leading reason why projects fall behind schedule	It's no surprise that issues are a leading reason that schedules are not met. Ideally, better upstream planning will minimize downstream issues; however, some issues will always persist. To keep your project on track, you need to systematically track and resolve issues.

Integration

Status reporting	A summary of the issues captured in this process should be integrated into the project's periodic status reports.
Action items	An issue is not a task or an action item. However, as part of your issue resolution plan, one or more action items may be assigned. These should be added to the action item list, while the core issue should remain on the issues list. See the *Action Item Tracking Process* in Appendix C for details.

Using the Issue Tracking Template

Done	Put a checkmark in the Done column and gray-out the row when an issue has been resolved. Move the whole row to the bottom of the table to keep only open issues visible at the top.
Issues	Provide a name and short description of the issue.
Priority	Assign a priority to the issue, such as High, Medium, or Low. This will enable the reader to quickly identify the high-priority issues. If needed, you can sort the entire list of issues by priority.

Owner	Assign ownership for resolving the issue to an individual.
Date logged	Enter the date that the issue was added to the issue list. If needed, you can sort the entire list by the date on which issues were logged.
Date due	Assign a target date for resolution of the issue.
Notes	Enter any comments or plans for resolution of the issue, such as the general approach and specific action items that have been assigned.

[Project Name] Issues

Done	Issues	Priority (H-M-L)	Owner	Date Logged	Date Due	Notes
	Issue #2	M	Wilson	May 3	Jun 5	Enter comments here
	Issue #5	M	Price	May 15	Jun 10	Enter comments here
Closed issues:						
√	Issue #1	M	Chin	May 3	May30	Enter comments here
√	Issue #3	L	Smith	May 5	May 22	Enter comments here
√	Issue #4	M	Smith	May 12	Jun 20	Enter comments here

Project Logo

APPENDIX C

ACTION ITEM TRACKING PROCESS

Systematically identifying, tracking, and completing action items is critical to advancing any project. Action items are the second-class citizens of project management that often get relegated to scribbles in the margin of your pad or on Post-it notes. This process describes a method for efficiently tracking action items by integrating their management with that of the (more prominent) tasks that appear on the project Gantt chart. An electronic copy of this process and template can be downloaded from www.xocp.com.

Definitions

Overview	There are many nuances in the way project managers define and treat action items and tasks. A strict definition may make *action items* and *tasks* synonymous; however, for the purposes of agile PM and this workflow, we will adopt the following definitions:
Task	A task is an undertaking assigned during the *planning* stage of the project and appears as a line item on the Gantt chart. An undertaking that is assigned during the *execution* stage is an action item until it is added to the Gantt chart, at which time it becomes a task.
Action item	An action item is an undertaking that gets assigned during the project execution phase (versus the planning

stage) and is generally too small to warrant being added to the formal project Gantt chart, yet still needs to get done in order for the project to advance. If an action item is eventually added to the Gantt chart, it can be removed from the action item list.

Action items often get assigned at meetings where issues are being discussed. Spontaneous brainstorming on issue resolution often happens so fast that formal planning is unnecessary or would be unproductive. In these cases, the issue resolution is accomplished by an organized sequence of action items.

Why We Track Action Items

Maintain visibility	One of the most valuable contributions that a project manager can make is simply to keep all key project indicators visible. Once projects leave the planning phase and enter the execution phase, things can start to get very chaotic. Providing and maintaining a single action item list for the team can be invaluable.
Organization	Action items are usually critical to moving the project forward, even though they do not appear on the formal project plan. Organized tracking of action items is necessary to keep this key element of project management under control.

Integration

Action items and tasks	As mentioned previously, action items and tasks are very similar. As such, it is efficient to have an integrated system to track them together, instead of maintaining two separate systems or lists. Developing simple systems to integrate these administrative duties will free up valuable time for more pressing responsibilities.

Organization of Template (three alternatives)

Action items and tasks are fully integrated	Ideally, both action items and tasks should be managed together in a single document. This allows for better sorting capabilities and efficiency. For instance, sorting information according to a particular time period would yield a sequential list of all action items and tasks due in that period. This is an excellent way to track project details. Updates to this document should be linked to up-

	dates in the Gantt chart. A fully integrated document can be cumbersome to manage manually, but it can be easily accomplished using specialized project management software.
Action items and tasks are partially integrated	Alternatively, the template can be divided into two sections: one for action items and the other for tasks. The columns are the same for both sections, so it is easy to correlate the data. Having one document with two distinct sections (as illustrated in the example template) makes this process easier to manage manually, but you will still have to reference the two different sections of the report. I find that this is the best solution for organizations without specialized PM software.
Action items only	Finally, you could decide to use this list, or one like it, to manage only action items. Tasks would be managed using the Gantt chart. However, this approach requires two different documents (and software programs), which increases the chances of one or the other not being current at any given time, or team members not always having the same versions of each document.

Using the Action Item and Tasks Template

Template reference	The example template included with this workflow is used when action items and tasks *are partially integrated,* as described above. The template and process can be modified, if necessary, to address the alternative scenarios.
Done	Put a checkmark in the Done column and gray-out the row when an action item or task has been completed. Move the whole row to the bottom of the section to keep only open action items or tasks visible at the top.
Action item or task	Provide a name and short description of the action item or task. For tasks, this data can be pulled directly from the Gantt chart.
Priority	Assign a priority to the action item or task, such as High, Medium, or Low. This will enable the reader to quickly identify the high-priority line items. If needed, you can sort the list of open action items or tasks by priority.
Owner	Assign ownership for completing the action item or task to an individual. For tasks, this data can be pulled directly from the Gantt chart.

Date logged	Enter the date that the action item or task was added to the list. If needed, you can sort the list of open action items or tasks by the date on which they were logged. For tasks, this is the start date on the Gantt chart.
Date due	Assign a target date for completion of the action item or task. For tasks, this is the finish date on the Gantt chart.
Notes	Enter any comments or plans related to the action item or task.

[Project Name] Action Items and Tasks

Done	Issues	Priority (H-M-L)	Owner	Date Logged	Date Due	Notes
	Action item #2	M	Wilson	May 3	Jun 5	Enter comments here
	Action item #5	M	Price	May 15	Jun 10	Enter comments here
✓	Action item #1	M	Chin	May 3	May 30	Enter comments here
✓	Action item #3	L	Smith	May 5	May 22	Enter comments here
✓	Action item #4	M	Smith	May 12	Jun 20	Enter comments here

Done	Tasks (from timeline)	Priority	Owner	Date Logged	Date Due	Notes
	Task #1		Chin	May 3	May 9	Enter comments here
	Task #2		Kane	May 7	May 25	
✓	Task #3		Smith	May 14	Jun 12	Enter comments here
✓	Task #4		Mac	May 24	Jun 18	
✓	Task #5		Chin	Jun 1	Jun 20	

Project Logo

APPENDIX D

PORTFOLIO PRIORITIZATION PROCESS

Portfolio prioritization needs to happen periodically to ensure that the business maintains its focus on the highest-priority projects and that they remain staffed for success. At any given time, a business may be running numerous projects simultaneously. These projects should be aligned into programs that support the business objectives and strategy. Businesses operating in an environment of uncertainty can expect frequent changes in the direction of both the business and individual projects. Without periodic efforts to reprioritize the project portfolio, we run the risk of wasting time and resources pursuing the wrong projects.

This process is meant to be used in conjunction with the Project Prioritization template and the Program View example, both of which are also provided in this appendix. An electronic copy of this process can be downloaded from www.xocp.com.

Project Prioritization

Align programs and projects with current strategy

Start with your most recent copy of the Program View diagram.

1. Verify the status and placement of all projects and programs currently on the diagram.

2. Remove any completed projects.

3. Add any new projects under the appropriate program and business objective. If a new (or old) project doesn't seem to fit under any current programs or business objectives, then create a "Misc." column and file them there for now.

4. Move and/or consolidate projects as appropriate.

5. Ensure that you reflect any moves or consolidation activities on the Project Data Sheets for the respective projects.

The output of this step is an up-to-date Program View and Project Data Sheet (PDS) for all projects.

The program and project managers should do this work offline (i.e., independent from the management team).

Update the resource estimate	Once you have updated the Project Data Sheets for all projects, you have current information from which to update the resource estimates at both the project and portfolio levels. An example of project-level resource estimation can be found in Chapter 7, and an example of portfolio-level resource estimation can be found in Chapter 11.
Identify your prioritization criteria	Work with the management team to identify the criteria that will be used to prioritize the projects. The criteria should reflect the business strategy. They should be expressed in tangible terms. Examples are: 1. Probability of technical success 2. Planned completion in next quarter/month 3. Supports ABC business objective 4. Is critical to getting new business
Assign a scoring method to each criteria	For each individual criterion, assign a noncomplex scoring method that will be used later for voting on the respective projects. Example scoring methods would be High-Medium-Low, or Yes-No, or a rating scale of 1 to 5. Whatever scoring method you decide on, you should be as consistent as possible in using it on all criteria. For example, do not rank one criterion on a scale of 1–10 and the others as H-M-L, because this will make tabulating the final scores more complicated. Once you decide on your scoring method, you can add it your criteria as follows:

1. Probability of technical success (H-M-L)
2. Planned completion in next quarter/month (H-M-L)
3. Supports ABC business objective (Y-N)
4. Is critical to getting new business (H-M-L)

You may assign a numeric score to any qualitative scoring methods, such as High = 3, Medium = 2, Low = 1 to normalize the criteria for easier comparison, if necessary.

Identify any go/ no-go thresholds	Identify any thresholds that will eliminate a project. Examples of thresholds may be:

1. No projects with a low probability of technical success
2. No projects requiring additional funds above $X
3. No projects with projected completion dates more than X months out

Thresholds should map to a particular score for a criterion.

Build the project prioritization matrix	Complete the Project Prioritization template by listing the projects (organized by program) down the left column and the criteria across the top.
Quantitative vote	Hold a prioritization meeting of project managers, technical leaders, management, and other key contributors who should have an influence on the prioritization effort. For each project, you should hold a vote on each criterion. This exercise prompts a lot of discussion, which should be encouraged since whole new perspectives on the project portfolio may be discovered. Record a single result from each vote. Try to facilitate the discussion to reach a consensus. If you can't gain unanimous agreement, then adopt the policy that the majority rules.
Break (optional)	This may be a good time for a break in the process. A time-out will let the facilitator update some of the materials before leading the team through the rest of the prioritization process. However, a break is not required or may not be desirable, especially if it would interrupt the group momentum.
Tabulate the quantitative score	Once the vote is completed, tabulate the score for each project using the scoring method previously defined. Record the score for each project on the Project Prioritization template and add the score to each project on the Program View diagram. Identify any projects that do not

	meet minimum thresholds and therefore should be eliminated or postponed.
Identify understaffed projects	Review the previously updated resource matrix and identify any understaffed projects. Identify them on the prioritization matrix and Program View diagram.
Qualitative adjustment	Have the team take a look at the newly updated Program View diagram, which should now have quantitative scoring and any resource deficiency assigned to each project. Since our quantitative scoring model is relatively unsophisticated, don't expect it to put the projects in perfect prioritized order. The team should take this opportunity to express their "gut feeling" on the results of the quantitative scoring. Go through each project, and discuss the current score. Decide as a group whether the score should stand or be adjusted upward or downward. Record the qualitative adjustments on the prioritization matrix and Program View diagram.
Assess new prioritization	Review the newly prioritized Program View to ensure that the highest-priority projects are staffed adequately for success. Decide if any projects should be postponed or canceled. Moving a project "below the line" is a difficult task, but it is something that may greatly enhance the chance of success for the remaining projects.
Prioritization complete	At this point, the project prioritization is complete. You should have a Program View diagram updated with a numerical score assigned to each project. You may want to highlight the "top 10" projects on the diagram to give them additional visibility.

Portfolio View Example

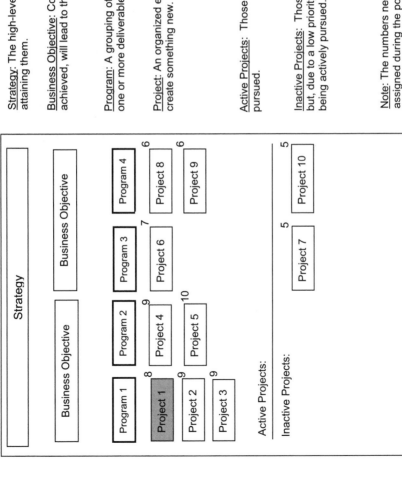

Strategy

Business Objective

Business Objective

Business Objective

Program 1

Program 2

Program 3

Program 4

Project 1 — 8
Project 4 — 9
Project 6 — 7
Project 8 — 6

Project 2 — 9
Project 5 — 10
Project 9 — 6

Project 3 — 9

Active Projects:

Inactive Projects:

Project 7 — 5
Project 10 — 5

Strategy: The high-level goals of the business and approach for attaining them.

Business Objective: Concrete deliverables and/or milestones that, once achieved, will lead to the attainment of the business strategy.

Program: A grouping of projects that, together, will lead to fulfillment of one or more deliverables/milestones required of a business objective.

Project: An organized effort to solve a problem, reach a milestone, or create something new.

Active Projects: Those projects that are staffed and actively being pursued.

Inactive Projects: Those projects that are critical to long-term success but, due to a low priority, are not able to be staffed and thus are not being actively pursued.

Note: The numbers next to the projects indicate the quantitative score assigned during the portfolio prioritization process.

Project Prioritization Template

	Supports ABC bus. objective (H-M-L)	Planned completion in current quarter (Y-N)	Critical to get new business (H-M-L)	Probability of technical success (H-M-L)	Score: L=1, M=2, H=3 Y=1, N=0	Scoring adjustments	Total score
Program 1							
Project 1	H	Y	M	M	8		8
Project 2	H	Y	M	H	9		9
Project 3	M	Y	M	M	7	+2	9
Program 2							
Project 4	M	Y	H	M	8	+1	9
Project 5	M	Y	H	H	9	+1	10
Program 3							
Project 6	M	Y	L	H	7		7
Project 7	L	N	L	H	5		5
Program 4							
Project 8	M	N	L	H	6		6
Project 9	M	N	L	H	6		6
Project 10	L	N	L	H	5		5

INDEX

ABOUT THE AUTHOR

Gary Chin is the founder of Cross Organizational (XO) Consulting, an independent firm helping organizations get started with project management, as well as attune it to their current business processes and corporate culture. He is also president of Personal Project Management Solutions, developing user-friendly PM applications that focus on the qualitative aspects of project definition/initiation and integrate execution stage activities with project planning. He has practiced, taught, and consulted in project management since 1985.

Gary holds a bachelor's degree in mechanical engineering from Rensselaer Polytechnic Institute, an MBA in marketing from Bentley College, PMP certification from the Project Management Institute, and is part of the American Management Association's Faculty in Project Management. He can be contacted at gchin@xocp.com.